ALSO BY SCOTT DOUGLAS

Meb for Mortals
Advanced Marathoning
The Little Red Book of Running

RUNNING

IS

MY

THERAPY

Relieve Stress and Anxiety, Fight Depression,
Ditch Bad Habits, and Live Happier

SCOTT DOUGLAS

THE EXPERIMENT

The Experiment, LLC | 220 East 23rd Street, Suite 600 | New York, NY 10010-4658
theexperimentpublishing.com

Many of the designations used by manufacturers and sellers to distinguish their products are claimed as trademarks. Where those designations appear in this book and The Experiment was aware of a trademark claim, the designations have been capitalized.

The Experiment's books are available at special discounts when purchased in bulk for premiums and sales promotions as well as for fund-raising or educational use. For details, contact us at info@theexperimentpublishing.com.

Library of Congress Cataloging-in-Publication Data

Names: Douglas, Scott, 1964- author.
Title: Running is my therapy : relieve stress and anxiety,
   fight depression, ditch bad habits, and live happier / Scott
   Douglas.
Description: New York : Experiment, 2018. | Includes bibliographical
   references.
Identifiers: LCCN 2018000558 (print) | LCCN 2018001846 (ebook) | ISBN
   9781615194452 (ebook) | ISBN 9781615194445 (pbk.)
Subjects: LCSH: Running--Psychological aspects. | Runners (Sports)--Mental
   health. | Runners (Sports)--Conduct of life.
Classification: LCC GV1061.8.P75 (ebook) | LCC GV1061.8.P75 D68 2018 (print)
   | DDC 613.7/172--dc23
LC record available at https://lccn.loc.gov/2018000558

ISBN 978-1-61519-444-5
Ebook ISBN 978-1-61519-445-2

Jacket and text design by Sarah Smith
Author photograph by Stacey Cramp

Manufactured in the United States of America

First printing April 2018

10 9 8 7 6 5 4 3 2 1

For everyone who runs to manage their mental health.
Let's keep going.

CONTENTS

In 2012, I rarely left my apartment. In part because I had no reason to—I was unemployed—and in part because I was generally unable to muster the courage to get out of bed. If you know me well today, you might be surprised to learn that back then, I spent most days on my bed, watching TV and surfing the internet aimlessly. When I was able to get my hands on Xanax, I would take four to six pills to fall into a deep sleep from which I secretly wished I would never wake, and when I was able to find only Nyquil, I took dozens of doses a day to calm my restless and ruminating mind.

I was depressed. My father was seven years into a Lewy body dementia diagnosis, which meant that he was a shell of the man I once knew. He was unable to walk, feed himself, or speak in coherent sentences, and because I was unemployed, I shared responsibility for taking care of him when my mother was at work. I was also fresh out of a painful relationship that I'd stayed in for far too long. After many years of hurt and disappointment, I ended things with my partner, which only led me into a deeper, all-consuming depression.

It's hard for me to reflect on this time without tearing up. I'd become so socially isolated that I rarely saw friends or family—even my roommate hardly knew I was there. I was certain that I was the unhappiest person on Earth; there couldn't possibly be anyone as miserable as I was.

Amid all this self-loathing, though, a bright spot emerged. A friend had signed up for a marathon, and I'd been watching his journey unfold on Facebook, and what struck me was that he was not your "typical runner" (he was black and not stick thin). Yet that wasn't stopping him, and his training seemed to be transforming his life. Because he was so unlike what I felt a marathon runner looked like and much closer to a "mortal" like me (at the time, I couldn't run a mile without stopping), I began to think that maybe I could (and should) run a marathon, too. I had nothing to lose, so I signed up and, in exchange for fundraising for The Leukemia and Lymphoma Society, received my first training plan.

Over the next sixteen weeks, I found myself putting up mileage I never thought possible. And as I grew into a "runner," I found that running was helping me more profoundly than I could ever have imagined. Running was not only offering me a means of catharsis, it was also opening me up to new experiences and new ways of thinking. For example, running became one of my most effective tools to help me cope with my father's worsening dementia. Knowing that he was slipping away more and more every day was a frightening fact I felt powerless against. Running restored some sense of control. If I couldn't halt his dementia, I could at least be in full charge of my running regimen: my mileage, speed, distance, and route. And when I stuck to my training plan, I found evidence of real results—I could run faster, farther, and with greater ease. It was also the first time there seemed to be a direct connection between effort and improvement. I was hooked, and as I grew more committed to the sport, I joined tune-up races before the marathon and started to set increasingly more challenging fitness goals for myself—and crushed them.

After completing my first marathon and raising more than $5,000 for the Leukemia and Lymphoma Society, I knew that running could save me from my depression. I'd found meaning, purpose, and pride in being able to help others while also helping myself. Today, running is my time to reflect on the challenges I face and the ways I might positively work through them, and it's my daily reminder that I have the power to change the circumstances of my life for the better. If and when I'm particularly anxious, the inherent repetition of running allows me to focus inward and find peace—it's meditation on the move. I almost always finish a run feeling better mentally, often with a renewed sense that I can tackle my life's problems.

And perhaps most important, I don't feel alone in my struggles anymore. When I founded the running movements Harlem Run (an NYC-based social-action running movement) and Run 4 All Women (an organization devoted to empowering women through fitness, also based in New York), I discovered a community of like-minded runners who find the same fulfillment through running that I do. Leading these groups, I've gotten to know hundreds of fellow runners in person and thousands more supporters from around the world on social media. Again and again, they tell me that running has inspired them to take action to change their lives. That keeps me going.

In my darkest moments, I wished that there were some easy cure for me to feel better. I wanted someone to prescribe the perfect dosage or the magic number of therapy hours I would need to finally be happy. I would spend hours fantasizing about going on a journey of self-discovery at an expensive rehab facility, the way that I imagined celebrities did, and coming out the other side a new person. Of course, no such easy fix exists. Instead, I stumbled upon running, which gave me the means to manage my depression; all I had to do was put in the work. And the work continues, with a dynamic and multi-pronged approach: I seek counseling regularly, I take medication when it's prescribed, and I always get my miles in.

And now, I have this book, one I only wish I'd had sooner. *Running Is My Therapy* presents the scientific evidence and anecdotes that confirm what I've discovered from my own experience: Running has a profoundly positive impact on your brain, and it can play a critical role in managing depression and anxiety—for some, it might even be all the treatment that's needed. May this book help you uncover your own road to better mental health through running.

Most Tuesdays, I run early in the morning with a woman named Meredith. For such close friends, we're quite different. Meredith is a voluble social worker who draws energy from crowds. I'm an introverted writer and editor who works from home. Meredith runs her best in large races and loves training with big groups. I've set personal records (PRs) in solo time trials and tend to bail when a run's head count gets above five. Meredith is a worrier, beset by regrets and worries, who has sought treatment for anxiety. I have dysthymia—chronic low-grade depression. We like to joke that Meredith stays up late to avoid the next day, whereas I go to bed early to speed the arrival of a better tomorrow.

We do have one key thing in common: Meredith and I run primarily for our mental health. Since our teens, we've leaned on regular running to improve the underlying fabric of our lives—our friendships, our marriages, our careers, our odds of being something other than miserable most of the time. Sure, we race, we enjoy the basic motion of running, and we appreciate being fit, lean, and in good physical health.

But the main draw of our seventy-five-minute prework loop is that we finish it feeling as if we've hit reset and can better handle the rest of the day.

Finishing a run in a better mood is a near-universal experience. It's so common, in fact, that you can buy T-shirts and mugs that read RUNNING IS MY THERAPY. Many people list psychological benefits among their top reasons to run. For those of us with depression or anxiety, however, our relationship to the mental side of the sport is often deeper. We view running's brain benefits the same way that cardiac patients might especially value running's effect on heart health.

The daily boosts are wonderful and welcome, but not the whole picture. Experts are still working out the explanation to what Meredith and I and millions of others have discovered—without regular running, our psychological set point will plummet.

I was diagnosed with dysthymia in 1995, soon after I turned thirty. What I described to the psychiatrist that day, however, had been a regular presence in my life since my teens. Starting in middle school, the unease I'd felt as a child gelled into what began to feel like basic aspects of my personality: low-grade disappointment about how little pleasure life delivers in comparison to the work it requires; pining for but seldom finding meaning in events and relationships; having to rally myself to find the mental and physical energy just to tend to daily affairs.

One of the great blessings of my life is discovering running soon after these symptoms took up residence. In the spring of 1979, as a ninth grader, I started running to prepare for high school cross-country the following fall. I was immediately hooked. Running was the first thing that combined day-to-day pleasure with the feeling of working toward something meaningful.

It took me a while to be able to appreciate and articulate just how profoundly running improved my life by improving my mental health. Depression wasn't openly discussed when I was in school. What little that was said about it had more to do with incapacitating episodes; as a good student who ran at least seventy miles a week, I saw little of myself in that presentation. For many years I went about my business, running a lot because it was the highlight of most of my days and because I sensed it uniquely girded me.

During that time I was able to nudge my way into running journalism. Since the early 1990s I've written hundreds of articles, primarily for *Runner's World* and the now-defunct *Running Times*, I've held editorial positions at both publications, and I've written or cowritten several running books. Being immersed in the industry has also meant reading or at least being aware of pretty much everything else that's written about running. As the years went by I waited for someone to write a book about running and mental health from the perspective of a lifelong runner. It didn't happen. Mental-health issues remain underexplored in running culture; that's odd given the frankness with which runners talk about bodily functions and similar matters with each other.

So, I decided to write the book myself. Such a book, I told myself, should articulate for fellow runners what "running is my therapy" means in our marrow. Such a book, I also told myself, should be interesting and useful for all levels of runners. In my view, if you run, you're a runner. There are no entry standards, no set number of miles per week or pace per mile, no given motivations or goals you have to have to count as a "real runner." Although you'll see me use personal examples of distance and intensity throughout this book, they're just that, personal examples, not prescriptions. While reading them, you'll probably recast them in your own equivalents. Again, to be a runner, you just have to run.

That said, most of the mental-health benefits we'll look at in this book happen only with regular running. Averaging at least two runs per week is a good, doable threshold to gain enough fitness so that every run isn't a challenge. If you struggle with consistency, or are just getting started as a runner, there are many excellent books, including Pete Magill's *The Born Again Runner*, on the nuts and bolts of beginning running.

I've long thought that runners with mental-health issues have an advantage over our sedentary counterparts. That's not just for the obvious reason that, through luck or pluck, we've already woven regular exercise into the fabric of our lives. As we'll see, a consistent running program is considered an effective stand-alone treatment for some types of depression and anxiety. It's also now known that regular running causes changes in the brain similar to those associated with antidepressant medications. And a lot of research has shown that exercise done in conjunction with typical treatments produces better results than the treatments done in isolation.

But there's another way in which we runners have an advantage. Regular running encourages and helps inculcate certain ways of thinking and behaving. It turns out that these habits of mind and body are strongly connected to common interventions for depression and anxiety, such as talk therapy, cognitive behavioral therapy, strong social connections, and good self-care practices. Our advantage here is twofold: First, we naturally practice some of these techniques as runners, thereby enjoying some of the *benefit* on our own. Second, being at least slightly familiar with various forms of treatment makes success with them more likely if we decide to seek professional help.

That's why this book is organized as it is. We'll start with detailed overviews of how running helps the brain, how it benefits people with depression and anxiety over the long run, and what's behind the day-to-day improvements in mood that are one of running's great calling cards. Then, we'll look at the intersection of running and several forms of treatment for depression and anxiety. To do all of that, we'll meet several people who, like me, have found running to be singularly effective in managing their mental health. We'll also hear from a wide range of experts, most of whom are runners, to explain the what and why behind my and others' experiences. We'll also see summaries of a decent amount of research on the many topics this book covers. (You'll see an endnote number after most study citations; in the back of the book you'll find the study's title and where to read it online.)

I don't want to give the impression that running solves everything. I'm never going to be a skipping-down-the-street kind of guy (except when I amuse the neighbors by doing running form drills). What running has done for me for almost four decades, and what I hope it will do the rest of my life, is to help me more often be my best—interested in rather than dismissive of others, engaged in rather than beaten down by work, hopeful rather than fearful toward the future. The time I spend running is powerful medicine not just while I'm running but for most of the rest of the day, too. If this book helps you to understand and appreciate a little better the role of running in your mental health, it will have been worth both of our time.

CHAPTER 1

How Running Helps Your Brain

The name of the running shoe brand Asics is an acronym for the Latin phrase *anima sana in corpore sano*. The literal translation is "a healthy soul in a healthy body." I don't have the original Greek handy, but Plato was getting at a similar point when he wrote, "The greatest mistake in the treatment of diseases is that there are physicians for the body and physicians for the soul, although the two cannot be separated."

It's long been understood that physical and mental health go together. Although our mind (or soul, to the ancients) is more than our brain, you need a well-functioning brain to have a vibrant mind. It's odd, then, when people don't think that their brain needs the same care and consideration accorded to other body parts. Experience and a growing body of research show that regular physical exercise is just as beneficial for your brain as it is for your heart, muscles, bones, and every other part of your body.

The bulk of this book is about the integration of body and mind via running for help in managing depression and anxiety. But that essential body-mind link is pertinent to everyone, regardless of the particulars of their mental health. So, before we look in depth at running, depression, and anxiety, let's start with some of the most important evidence for how exercise is necessary for optimal brain health.

THE SMART RUNNER

We runners like to think we're smart because we run. And we are, if "smart because we run" means we're smart to run, given the mountain of evidence on how running improves health and vitality while reducing the risk for heart disease, diabetes, high blood pressure, stroke, some types of cancer, and other diseases. One large long-term study even found that runners are at lower risk of developing cataracts.[1]

But "smart because we run" can be taken even more literally, in the sense of smarter than we otherwise would be. Research overwhelmingly shows that people who regularly do aerobic exercise, such as running, perform better on several types of cognitive tasks.[2] To flip the equation, research shows that, on average, sedentary people do worse in several common measures of cognitive performance.[3]

Jeffrey Burns, MD, is a six-time marathoner, brain researcher, and professor of neurology at the University of Kansas. He acknowledges that a runners-are-smarter message might have a chicken-or-egg quality to it. "From a scientific perspective, we know that smart people exercise and that people who exercise tend to be smarter to start with," he says. "We have dozens if not hundreds of studies showing that exercise is associated with smartness, but we don't necessarily know if that's because smart people exercise or exercise makes us smarter."

Burns says it's probably a combination of both. On an individual level, what matters is improvement within your range of inherent intellect. Running an hour a day isn't going to put me anywhere near the intellectual level of wheelchair-bound Stephen Hawking. But all evidence is that my mileage makes for a smarter Scott than if I were sedentary.

Consider experiments in which half a group of people start an aerobic exercise program and the other half remain sedentary. After as little as six weeks of regular workouts, the exercisers improve their performance on several mental tests, including working memory (the ability to temporarily store and use information needed to carry out a task) and visuospatial processing (the ability to perceive and interact with what you see around you).[4] There's also good evidence that getting fit improves attentional focus, which is the ability to focus on relevant cues in an environment while working toward a goal. I remind myself how attentional focus differs from more general focus by thinking about trail running: Attentional focus is surveying the ground I'll encounter in the next few strides to make sure I don't trip. When, instead, I focus on finding edible mushrooms or locating owls in trees, I frequently fail to meet the goal of staying upright.

"What's been most consistently linked to exercise is executive function," Burns says. "That's the ability to plan and organize, to take in information and act on it. That's a really important part of day-to-day life—taking in a lot of information and making goal-oriented decisions and planning. The best example of executive function is something like putting together Thanksgiving dinner, where you've got fifty ingredients and ten things you're making, and the timing of everything is different but needs to end at the same time."

Task juggling à la Burns' Thanksgiving dinner example has long been my favorite part of working, from waiting tables to editing *Runner's World*'s daily news channel. It's a fun challenge to see how many things with different timelines I can keep moving forward. This is not multitasking. It's been pretty well established that doing several things at once—emailing one person and texting another while participating in a conference call—reduces your performance on each task. Executive function is better understood as focusing on one thing for the time it requires while not inhibiting the progress of the other tasks you have in motion. It's nice to think that being a runner made me better at most of the jobs I've had.

HOW RUNNING HELPS YOUR BRAIN   25

If, instead, you find yourself in a situation requiring sustained focus on one thing, you'll still probably do better if you're a runner. That's a reasonable conclusion to make from the available research, such as a Spanish study that found aerobically fit subjects performed better than sedentary people on a test of sustained mental focus.[5]

For the study, researchers gathered twenty-two triathletes, who trained eight or more hours a week, and twenty people whom they classified as having low aerobic fitness. The subjects performed a dull but demanding task for one hour. Sitting in front of a black computer screen, they were to react as quickly as possible when they saw a full red circle, which appeared at intermittent intervals. The average test involved reacting to about four hundred circles.

The researchers measured the subjects' reaction times and brain activity in twelve-minute segments during the one-hour test. In the first thirty-six minutes, the triathletes had quicker reaction times than the less-fit subjects. Throughout the test, the triathletes' brains showed greater brain activity associated with allocating mental resources to a task, as well as brain activity associated with a preparatory response to a task. Taken together, the researchers wrote, the results "demonstrated a positive association between aerobic fitness, sustained attention, and response preparation."

"Sustained attention is the ability to maintain performance over a long period of time, which depends on maintaining vigilance, the ability to detect the stimulus, and resistance to distraction," Antonio Luque-Casado, PhD, the lead author of the study, told me in an email. "A reduced ability to monitor significant sources of information directly affects all cognitive abilities (i.e., slow responses and/or failures to respond to target stimuli). Therefore, sustained attention is an inherent function [of] general cognitive performance that is critical to cognitive abilities in humans." Luque-Casado said that being able to sustain mental attention is important in both everyday activities, such as driving or absorbing a presentation at work, and intricate professional tasks, such as performing surgery or handling air traffic control.

The general exercise-makes-you-smarter good news appears to be true throughout life. Research has found better cognitive performance among fit people whether they're school-aged, younger adults, middle-aged, or older adults.[6] These running-makes-you-smarter findings generally have to do with mental acuity during our sedentary hours. But what about when we're running?

GET RUNNING, GET CREATIVE

Research backs what you've probably noticed—your brain seems to kick things up a notch once you're in a running groove. A Dutch study published in 2013 found that regular exercisers performed better on a creative problem-solving test when they did a short workout.[7] The research involved ninety-six people, half of whom were sedentary and half of whom exercised at least three times a week over the previous two years. Half of each group did two types of mental tasks while at rest, and the other half of each group did the tasks while riding a stationary bike.

The tasks measured two key components of creativity: divergent thinking and convergent thinking. Divergent thinking is used to generate many new ideas when more than one solution is correct; this is (ideally) what happens during a brainstorming session. In the study, for example, participants were asked to come up with as many uses as possible for a pen (write a note, drum on a table, give as a gift, make a new belt hole because you've lost so much weight, etc.).

Convergent thinking, in contrast, is used to come up with one good solution to a problem. As an example, the study participants were presented with three unrelated words (e.g., *hair*, *time*, and *stretch*) and asked to think of an associated word common to the three (in this case, long).

As expected, the regular exercisers did better than the sedentary people in both types of tasks. The most noteworthy result was that the fit people did better on the convergent-thinking test while exercising than when at rest. This might not surprise anyone who's had an "Aha!" moment ten minutes into a run after mulling a problem all day, but it's nice to see the phenomenon backed by research. The nonfit people, meanwhile, performed worse when cycling than when at rest; the researchers speculate that the unaccustomed activity taxed their brains enough to impair concentration. The researchers wrote, "From the current results, one may even speculate that for people who are used to exercise, the absence of exercise . . . impairs [creative] performance more than its presence improves it."

Burns is familiar with this phenomenon. He walked while we talked to better collect his thoughts, and he explained that running helps his writing. "When I'm out running," he said, "sentences will pop into my head and they sort of come together in a new way. The ideas or new ways of thinking tend to bubble up and appear without effort when I've been working hard and not getting them in my usual environment." Burns says he doesn't have a sound explanation for why this happens, but, in his expert opinion, "it's cool." For my part, much of this book was hashed out in my head while running the trails of Cape Elizabeth, Maine. The steady beat of my footsteps induces a sense of rhythm that lets me hear how sentences in a paragraph should flow. It's much rarer for the words to just fall into place when I'm sitting in my home office, urging thoughts to organize themselves while trying to block out distractions.

Burns and I learned long ago something else discovered by the convergent-thinking researchers. The creative boost from working out for the regular exercisers was temporary. As the researchers put it, "The enhancement of cognitive-control processes by aerobic fitness is so short-lived that positive effects are restricted to performance during or directly after exercising." Burns says, "When I get home from a run, I have to write it down right away or it's gone. It's like waking up from a dream." Here's the one life hack you'll read in this book: On those happy occasions when the way out of a writing maze or the solution to NPR's Sunday puzzle appears six miles into a run, I move my wedding band to my right ring finger. Otherwise, the thought will slither away as suddenly as it appeared. When I get home, seeing the ring on the wrong hand reminds me of my breakthrough.

Not all runs are created equal when it comes to getting this immediate boost in smarts. You've probably done an especially long or hard workout and, for the next few hours, not been able to think much beyond "I like food. Kittens are cute." Over the course of my highest mileage week of my life, 184 miles, my cognitive threshold went from reading Shakespeare's *Richard II* to watching cable news.

"When it comes to highly exhaustive exercise, yes, there's a refractory period," J. Carson Smith, PhD, a brain researcher and kinesiology professor at the University of Maryland, says. "You need to recover. There is evidence that you can impair cognitive function with high-intensity exercise—your attention has a limited capacity." With long runs, Smith says, "you're depleting your glycogen stores," which are your muscles' stored form of carbohydrate. "Your brain needs glycogen to function well. You need to rehydrate, replenish glycogen stores. It's not surprising that people who train intensely for long periods of time need some time for a recovery period."

As Smith points out, three-hour runs and long, hard track workouts are more the exception than how most people run most of the time. Your standard getting-in-the-miles run at a moderate pace produces more of the immediate get-smart benefits, and those benefits "can occur much sooner after the workout ends," Smith says. There appears to be a sweet spot of longer-but-not-too-long: In one study, the immediate gains were similar after twenty- and forty-minute workouts, but half an hour later, the longer workouts seemed to impart more lasting effects.[8]

I don't want to make too big a deal about these immediate benefits. In addition to being transitory, the amount of effect is small to moderate. A conversational-pace five-miler will probably help me finish a Sudoku puzzle faster, but it isn't going to transform me into a chess master. What's really exciting is how these daily hits appear to help us age better.

A BETTER BRAIN IN THE LONG RUN

If you want to feel good about being a longtime runner, talk to brain researchers like Burns and Smith.

Now in my fifties, I like to think my decades of running have me in much better physical health than my high school and college classmates who have been sedentary since we were in school. Facebook photos at least superficially support this belief. So, hurray for running on that count. But not until I really delved into this topic did I appreciate just how much good my lifetime of running has presumably done on the cognitive side of things.

Burns, whose current research focuses on dementia and Alzheimer's disease, says, "Staying active and maintaining heart and lung function goes a long way toward promoting the long-term health of your brain. As we get older, we're all at risk of cognitive decline. In people who continue to exercise, we tend to see a slowing of that inevitable decline in some areas of cognition. The evidence certainly points to good cardiorespiratory fitness reducing your long-term risk of developing Alzheimer's disease, stroke, and cardiovascular disease." Two main factors are at play here: slowing or stopping the typical age-related loss in brain tissue, and better preserving the underlying structure of key brain areas, such as the frontal lobe (the key player in executive function) and hippocampus (where much work having to do with memory occurs).

These benefits, like a Sunday afternoon free of errands or a morning spent watching birds while sipping your coffee, are perhaps better appreciated with age. "If you're exercising in midlife, you're doing your brain a favor for the long term," Smith says. "That's something that young people tend not to be thinking about—being motivated to run today to help their brain when they're sixty or seventy. But we think if you start earlier and maintain longer, your benefits are probably greater."

Not that I plan to stop running anytime soon, and neither should you. But it's possible that some of the brain boost from years of running might stick around if you were forced to become sedentary. "We assume the cumulative effects of exercise provide some protection over time," Smith says. Entering middle age as someone who has run for several years "should build a cognitive reserve that as you continue on in life you can draw upon," he says. One study in this vein followed 2,700 people over a twenty-five-year period. It found that when the subjects were between forty-three and fifty-five years old, those with the greatest cardiovascular fitness a quarter-century before did better on tests of verbal memory (recalling a list of words) and psychomotor speed (physically reacting to a cognitive stimulus).[9]

At the other end of the spectrum, these brain-health benefits support the idea that it's never too late to start running. When older people begin an aerobic exercise program, "there's evidence that there are boosts to certain aspects of memory and thinking, as opposed to slowing or decline," Burns says. A review of research on exercise and cognitive function in older people concluded that "physical exercise is a promising nonpharmaceutical intervention to prevent age-related cognitive decline and neurodegenerative diseases."[10]

In an aging society, Burns' work is part of an important movement, and he's excited to conduct research on exercise and older people's brains. "Forty years ago, running and diet and exercise were not a part of how to go after heart disease," he says. "Now that's standard. We're kind of sitting where cardiology was forty years ago and leveraging what we think is true about lifestyle and its importance to brain health."

Those with a more-is-better mind-set will appreciate a key finding from Burns' research on both younger and older adults: The greatest gains in cognitive function were by the people who most improved their VO_2 max, the gold standard for measuring aerobic fitness. Your VO_2 max is the maximum amount of oxygen you can breathe in and deliver to working muscles during exercise. Runners have among the highest VO_2 maxes of all athletes. "An individual's cardiorespiratory fitness response was a better predictor of cognitive gains than exercise dose (i.e., duration) and thus maximizing an individual's cardiorespiratory fitness may be an important therapeutic target for achieving cognitive benefits," concludes a Burns study on previously sedentary people aged sixty-five or older.[11]

"It's not clear if it's the heart and lung function that's driving the brain benefits, or if it's that the people who achieve that increase in fitness level are achieving broad physiological benefits," Burns told me. "I think it does suggest that maybe we need to focus on ways to better boost cardiorespiratory fitness, and intensity is one way to do that. That's something our future studies will focus on: Do we need to do high-intensity training versus just moderate intensity focused on duration?"

As is my wont, I extrapolated from Burns' research to my situation. Is it reasonable, I asked, to think that, for those who are already fit, regularly including hard workouts is better for brain health than nothing but easy to moderate running? Even when you have no racing plans, should you do such workouts as eight-hundred-meter repeats at 5K race pace, which improve your VO_2 max more than conversational-pace runs?

"You're interpreting it the way we're thinking about it," Burns replied. (Bless him.) "The way I think about it from an exercise physiology standpoint is that the right target is to boost cardiorespiratory fitness. So, when we're designing a prescription for exercise, our goal should be to boost cardiorespiratory fitness for that person. Our data suggest that's necessary to achieve the brain benefits."

THE OXYGENATED BRAIN IS A HAPPY BRAIN

What's behind these improvements in cognitive functioning that, on the face of it, seem to have nothing to do with running? After all, when you do a very long run and draw down your leg muscles' glycogen supply, your body responds by improving your ability to deposit and hold on to these stores of carbohydrate. That's an example of adapting to a stress by anticipating the stress occurring again and rebuilding to better handle the next time it occurs. The body's typical stress-recover-adapt cycle doesn't seem to apply to something like an improved ability to focus on relevant items, especially when some of those improvements occur *while* you're running.

In the case of running-induced cognitive improvements, the benefit appears to be indirect. One view is that substances that the body produces more of in response to running happen to also lead to enhanced brain function. As one review of research on the topic puts it, "the areas of brain most influenced by aerobic fitness are higher-order regions involved in the control of cognition and memory." For example, muscles release a protein called cathepsin B after exercise to speed recovery. In 2016, researchers linked increased circulating levels of cathepsin B to greater production of a protein called brain-derived neurotrophic factor (BDNF).[12] As we'll see in greater detail later, BDNF contributes to the growth of more

neurons in the brain and increases in the size of the hippocampus. In a study that compared BDNF levels following distance running, resistance training, and high-intensity interval
training, the biggest increases came from distance running.
This makes sense if the cathepsin B theory is correct, because
the impact stress of distance running would likely spur the
muscles to release more of the protein for repair.

Any one specific mechanism, such as cathepsin B leading to BDNF increases, is only part of the organic whole of
you the runner. "The physiological changes of one bout of
exercise are profound and have an impact on every aspect
of you and your body," Burns says. Two of the more obvious changes during a run are increased blood pressure and
increased blood flow to the brain, leading to feeling more
alert. Increased brain blood flow "could certainly enhance
areas of the brain that are processing information," notes
Smith.

But, Smith is quick to add, the difficulty with understanding how running affects the brain is that it affects several
related systems at once. "You're getting increases in BDNF,
but also you're getting increases in other neurotransmitters,
such as norepinephrine, serotonin, and dopamine," he says.
"So, it's probably a combination of these types of neurotransmitters that are helping the reward-related circuitry of your
brain to function more effectively." In addition, Smith adds,
increased levels of substances such as norepinephrine modu-
late nerve cells in the brain. "They can help dampen the noise
and increase the gain on the signal you're trying to attain so

that the networks can better resolve the right decision more quickly, or the memory comes to mind more easily," he says. "All of those things come together and play a role."

It's perhaps even more complicated to tease out what causes the long-term benefits of running to brain health. "People argue over which one is most important," Burns says. "I think they're all important and they're all probably playing a role in providing these benefits to the brain."

Greater blood flow on a regular basis is one contributor. Healthier blood vessels "react appropriately to constrict and relax when needed to deliver blood to different parts of the brain," Smith says.

But what about other aspects of structural change? Luque-Casado told me that the attention required while running probably isn't the main driver behind his findings of endurance athletes performing better on tests of focus. Other researchers might disagree. Using MRIs to measure the brains of competitive runners and age-matched sedentary people, a University of Arizona study found that the runners had greater functional connectivity between separate parts of their brains.[13] The parts of the runners' brains that were wired differently are involved in the higher-level cognitive work we've seen elsewhere in this chapter, such as working memory, attentional focus, and processing speed.

In discussing their findings, the researchers suggested that regular running seems to rewire our brains. "High-intensity aerobic activity that requires sustained, repetitive locomotor and navigational skills may stress cognitive domains in ways that lead to altered brain connectivity," they wrote. Those of us who have been able to retrace an old running route for the first time in a decade can appreciate the idea that making our way through the world builds our brains in this way. As the Arizona researchers put it, "Enhanced connectivity may occur in response to cognitive demands during exercise, yet the strengthened connections may improve executive function more broadly, allowing for improved cognitive function later in life."

Another key to later-in-life brain health is running's role in lowering inflammation. Amyloid plaques are fibrous clumps of protein fragments that attach to the outside of cells and are thought to contribute to Alzheimer's and other cognitive problems. Smith and Burns agree that regular running can help to remove these plaques and other toxic substances from the brain.

Those potentially obscure-sounding things with names like brain-derived neurotrophic factor and norepinephrine play a huge role over time. Well-functioning neurotransmitter systems lead to "nothing really becoming overexpressed or not responding quickly enough," thus keeping the brain's system for responding to stress and other stimuli well regulated and in balance, Smith says. Improved function in and increased size of the hippocampus means that, with age, this key part of the brain can be protected somewhat, which in turns enhances overall brain function.

All of the above is much more than was known about the body-mind health connection when someone first said "*anima sana in corpore sano.*" Regular running has as profound an effect on your brain's health as it does on the body parts most people more often focus on. For those of us who run in part to manage our mental health, these benefits are even more noteworthy. Many of the positive changes here described—increased BDNF levels, better-functioning neurotransmitter systems, growth in the hippocampus—are key to running providing short- and long-term relief from depression and anxiety. That's the subject of the next few chapters.

CHAPTER 2

How Running Helps People with Depression

Say you woke one morning with ringing in your ears. The first thing you'd probably do is review recent events for a cause—you went to a concert, flew, ate in a loud restaurant, and so forth. If you couldn't discern a cause, you might wonder what's going on, and perhaps Google "sudden ringing in ears." The ringing might dominate your day, and then, in the likely event it soon went away, you'd forget about it.

If the ringing persisted for a few weeks, you'd probably get it checked out, even if you knew what had triggered it. If it then went away, you'd keep the incident in the back of your mind, and be more concerned if, later that year, you had another ringing episode.

If the ringing never went away, you'd realize you have tinnitus. You'd tell yourself it's going to be something to deal with the rest of your life. You'd develop coping strategies, experiment with ways to manage it, and try to get on with living your life. In your more self-pitying modes, if someone complained they had ringing in their ears after a long plane ride, you might think, "Try having it all the time, for no obvious reason."

That's one way of thinking about depression compared to the short periods of sadness, lethargy, and reduced interest in normal activities that everybody experiences. Living with depression means finding ways to manage it so that it interferes as little as possible. For many of us, being a runner is one of our key coping strategies. We feel intuitively what experts increasingly believe—that running not only helps us feel better but also has carryover benefits that can improve other aspects of our lives.

A QUICK OVERVIEW OF DEPRESSION

Although there's less stigma attached to depression and other mental-health disorders than there used to be, many people still struggle with discussing these issues openly. That's odd when you consider how prevalent depression is.

The World Health Organization says that depression is the leading cause of disability worldwide, including in the United States and Canada. The National Institute of Mental Health estimates that, in 2015, 16.1 million adults in the United States had at least one depressive episode. That figure represented 6.7 percent of the adult population at the

time and included only people who met the classic definition for a major depressive episode: a period of at least two
weeks during which they experienced a depressed mood and
at least four other symptoms indicating significant changes
in functioning (dramatic drop in energy, different sleeping
and eating patterns, difficulty concentrating, lower self-
esteem, decreased interest in normally pleasurable activities,
etc.). The number of people living with depression would be
higher if it included those with chronic depression as well as
children and teens. "I would say ten to fifteen percent of the
population at any time could be thought of as depressed,"
says Frank Brooks, PhD, a clinical social worker and professor in Portland, Maine. "So, in any year, that's more than
thirty million people in the US alone."

Offering a concise description of depression is difficult.
It's not a binary condition, like having a broken bone or being
pregnant. Clinicians look at a large number of symptoms
having to do with how people think, act, and feel. Gradations
of depression—mild, moderate, severe—can be a judgment
call. One well-known screen, the Mood and Feeling Ques-
tionnaire (MFQ), cautions users that "there are no prescribed
cut points" that unambiguously define the presence or severity of depression.

There's also great variance in how people experience
depression. I've never been suicidal, and I'm too vain to
respond with anything but "not true" to the MFQ potential
symptom "I could never be as good as other people." But to
other MFQ symptoms—"I felt miserable or unhappy" or "I

felt lonely" or "I didn't enjoy anything at all"—my first reaction is often, "What thinking person wouldn't feel that way?"

Further clouding clear categories is that many depression screenings have to do with recent feelings and behaviors, such as over the past two weeks. These more accurately capture depressive episodes, a somewhat sudden change in mood, behavior, energy level, and so on. There are also what are known as depressive disorders, in which symptoms are less severe but more persistent.

"It's tricky because if people have always had symptoms and it's been lifelong, they might not know any difference," Brian Vasey, MD, a clinical psychiatrist and runner from Madison, Wisconsin, says about diagnosing some people. Indeed, when I look at such screening statements as "I felt like talking less than usual" or "I was moving and walking more slowly than usual," I often think, "No, not more so than usual, but that's not saying much."

All that being the case, it can be more helpful to hear others' general descriptions of depression than offer an ironclad definition. Let's start with therapists.

"I would describe depression as a feeling of joylessness, meaninglessness, lack of motivation, lack of caring," Vasey says. "But it depends—people are different. Kids who are depressed can be angry and quite easily irritated. I've had people who say they felt like everyone is mean to them, and when the depression got better they felt like, 'Wow, people are being nice.' They didn't feel like their mood was better, but felt that people were treating them better."

Brooks emphasizes functioning in daily life—sleeping, going to work, meeting your normal responsibilities to yourself and others. "There's a profound difference between 'I'm having a bad day at work' and 'I'm having a bad day at work and I'm not going to get out of bed tomorrow because of it,'" he says. Brooks also hones in on how one's relationships are faring: "Even mild depression can have very, very significant effects on interpersonal relationships."

Vasey and Brooks agree with Laura Fredendall, PsyD, a clinical psychologist and runner from Terre Haute, Indiana, who says, "The duration of feelings and number of symptoms are the key to making a diagnosis. But I like to see the person as more than a representation of someone who has a depressive disorder." Vasey agrees: "It's all about the person in front of me and their relationships. It's 'Who are you?' rather than 'What are your symptoms?'"

What about runners with depression? I'll describe my early experiences with running and depression later in this chapter. Here are a few other runners' takes.

Kristin Barry, a lifelong runner from Scarborough, Maine, recalls first feeling depressed in middle school. "When it's not that bad, it's just a low-level sadness," she says. "Sometimes it's tiredness and a level of hopelessness, wondering why I can't feel like what seems like everyone else, but not at a crippling level." Barry had one severe episode in 1997, during her first year of law school. "I couldn't concentrate, felt despair and extreme hopelessness, didn't enjoy anything, and withdrew myself from just about everything."

Rich Harfst, of Annandale, Virginia, is another lifelong runner who has dealt with depression since his teens. A therapist gave him a diagnosis at age seventeen. "Because I was beginning to interact more with the external world, it started showing up in how I behaved at school and my part-time job," he says. "My parents thought I was going through some adjustment issues or teenage anger issues."

Now in his fifties, Harfst has experienced both chronic and episodic depression.

"I have some behaviors that are manic-depressive in nature, but my manic is very subdued," he reports. "I correct to a medium, but for me it's a pretty big high. I've had half a dozen periods in my life where, for one reason or another, I've sunk into a longer funk, on the order of six weeks."

Amelia Gapin, a software engineer from Jersey City, New Jersey, has also dealt with chronic and episodic depression, although the latter has improved since she became more dedicated to running. "There was always the underlying steady state of depression throughout the daily stuff that gets in the way," she says. "But then there was the episodic period when it would be really bad for six weeks, two months, where I couldn't even get myself out of bed. During the weekends it was: wake up and take a couple hours to move myself to the couch, and then just kind of stay there. People think depression is feeling bad, but a lot of times you just kind of feel nothing—you feel empty and drained of any emotion."

Given the great variance in how people experience depression, it's perhaps not surprising that its causes are still unclear.

The National Institute of Mental Health offers the sweeping explanation, "Current research suggests that depression is caused by a combination of genetic, biological, environmental, and psychological factors." To take just one example of the complexity of causes: Modern antidepressants address biological factors, such as deficits in the brain's serotonin system. But not everybody with such a deficit develops depression, and not everybody with depression displays unusual brain chemistry.

There's also no expert consensus on whether biological observations, such as shrinkage in the brain area known as the hippocampus, are a cause or a consequence of depression. One theory is what's known as kindling, in which a depressive episode alters the brain's structure or functioning in such a way that it's more vulnerable to subsequent life-event stressors. This interaction of biological and environmental factors might help explain why some people can have a major depressive episode after a stressful event, such as the death of a child, and then never be depressed again once they recover, whereas others can become incapacitated by comparatively minor stressors. Rich Harfst has had depressive episodes triggered by the end of romantic relationships, and Amelia Gapin had a major episode in the wake of gender transition surgery. No compassionate person would deny the reality of Harfst's and Gapin's suffering. But its existence after events that others experience without becoming depressed is a reminder of just how tricky ferreting out depression's causes can be.

Even the well-established family-history link can be difficult to untangle. A genetic component seems obvious on the face of it. But what about environmental and psychological factors, such as socioeconomic status and children's adopting their parents' ways of thinking and coping? As far as I know, none of my five siblings and neither of my parents have been diagnosed with depression. But one of my grandfathers received electroshock therapy for depression, indicating his condition was quite severe, given the shame attached to mental-health issues in the first half of the twentieth century. Did unfavorable brain chemistry skip two generations and then pass on only to me? Did my siblings reach fundamentally different conclusions about how to think about life from their observations of our parents? Who knows?

And not to be too glib, but to a certain extent, who cares? What really matters when you have depression is not why you have it, but what to do about it. That I'm the only runner in my family might not be a fluke. There's solid evidence supporting my decision to become one.

THE CASE FOR RUNNING AS A TREATMENT FOR DEPRESSION

Over the past couple of decades, there's been a growing body of research on exercise as a potential form of treatment for depression. (Almost all of this research uses aerobic exercise, of which running is a form, as the treatment. In chapter 4, we'll look in detail at whether running is singularly effective compared to other forms of exercise.) These studies tend to divide previously sedentary people with depression into two or more groups and see how various forms of treatment affect their depressive symptoms at the end of the study. Some studies have just two groups, a control group that remains sedentary and a group that begins an exercise program. Other studies compare exercise to common treatments, such as antidepressants and psychotherapy, while the control group receives a placebo.

For example, a famous Duke University study divided 202 adults with major depression into four groups receiving different treatment: supervised exercise in a group setting, unsupervised home-based exercise, the antidepressant sertraline (brand name Zoloft), or a placebo pill. The subjects' level of depression was retested at the end of the sixteen-week study. After the four months of treatment, 41 percent of the subjects no longer met the clinical standards for major depression, with this being the key detail: The two groups of exercisers improved as much as the people who took antidepressants.[1] (These groups all improved more than the control group.) In a follow-up study, the researchers checked in on the subjects one year after the end of the first study (i.e., sixteen months after the beginning of the first study). The researchers found that the people who continued to exercise regularly during that year had, on average, the biggest decrease in depressive symptoms.[2]

Studies such as these support the idea that exercise can be as effective as antidepressants in relieving symptoms of depression. This idea was bolstered by a review of research on the topic published in 2017.[3] In contrast to original research, such as the Duke University studies, research reviews look at all well-designed research on a topic to identify commonly reached conclusions. The 2017 review found that the Duke studies weren't a fluke. "All these studies reported that exercise and standard antidepressant treatments were equally effective," the review states.

The most well-known review of research on exercise for depression is called the Cochrane review.[4] Updated as new studies are done, it includes results from research on people with mild to moderate as well as major depression. The most recent version pools the results from thirty-nine studies, with a total of more than 2,300 subjects. Its main take-home finding for our purposes is that exercise was as effective as antidepressants and psychotherapy in reducing depressive symptoms. Other research supports using exercise in conjunction with other treatments.[5] The main types of those treatments are the subject of several later chapters.

There's also evidence that regular exercise can prevent developing depression.[6] A Norwegian study followed almost thirty-four thousand adults over a nine- to thirteen-year period. At the beginning of the study, none had symptoms of depression. During the study period, 7 percent of the subjects developed symptoms meriting a diagnosis of depression. The researchers also collected data on the subjects' exercise habits at the beginning and end of the study. Those who got no regular exercise were an astounding 44 percent more likely to develop depression than those who exercised for one to two hours a week. The design of the study is significant because by including only people who weren't depressed at the outset, it removed the possibility that subjects who were sedentary were that way because of depression. Another point concerning the link between being sedentary and depression: Inactivity increases the risk of developing common conditions, such as heart disease and diabetes, which might further the risk of developing depression.[7]

Despite the ever-growing amount of evidence for exercise as a treatment for depression, resistance remains. Some of the pushback against exercise as medicine stems from the reasonable point that you often can't get people to do it. According to the Centers for Disease Control and Population, only 21 percent of the US population gets the recommended 150 minutes (two and a half hours) of light to moderate aerobic exercise per week. It's also reasonable to point out that people suffering from depression might have an especially hard time getting themselves to work out for half an hour five days a week. But for many regular runners, these modest recommendations are probably not an issue. Fifteen miles a week at a pace of 10:00 per mile gets you to 150 minutes.

Another reason given for skepticism about exercise's efficacy is study methodology. Refuting that skepticism requires a brief detour on the topic of research in general.

The gold standard for peer-reviewed research is what's known as a double-blind study, in which neither the subjects nor the researchers know which subjects got which treatment. So, for example, when testing a new medication, you'd have half of the subjects get the medication and half get a placebo that's indistinguishable from the medication in terms of appearance, taste, and so on. You would distribute the medication such that the people taking and administering the medication couldn't tell who got the medication and who got the placebo. This design lessens the chance that perceptions of the medication's effects will influence the subjects' reactions to it and the researchers' interpretation of those reactions.

Double-blind studies are simply not possible for some areas of investigation, including exercise. If you're depressed and sedentary and agree to take part in a study on whether exercise reduces your depressive symptoms, you'll know whether you were part of the group that started exercising or whether you were in the control group that remained sedentary. You might then report feeling better after six weeks of working out because you've heard that exercise helps with depression; your expectation of a benefit might produce that benefit.

The phenomenon of getting better because you expect to get better is an example of the placebo effect. The phrase *placebo effect* is often used dismissively. For example, a runner's faster race times soon after switching to a new coach are said to be a placebo effect, because she couldn't have gotten that much fitter in two weeks. Researchers, in contrast, acknowledge the validity of the placebo effect. It's a powerful reminder of the role our mind plays in how our body feels. That's especially the case for depression, which isn't as easily diagnosed as a physical malady, such as kidney disease.

Researchers attempt to account for the placebo effect in designing studies. In testing a new medication, they'll expect some of the people who get the placebo to report some of the same effects as the people taking the medication. What they'll be looking for is whether the effects reported by the people taking the medication are significantly different (in both type and degree) from those reported by the placebo group.

In testing whether exercise helps people with depression, the placebo effect is accounted for by giving the sedentary control group an inefficacious pill. This method has been used for other forms of treatment where it's impossible to hide whether you're getting the treatment, such as talk therapy. The takeaway from this tutorial: In studies designed like this, the people who start exercising report more improvement than the control group.

In discussing an earlier version of the Duke University exercise-versus-Zoloft study, John Ratey, MD, writes in his book *Spark: The Revolutionary New Science of Exercise and the Brain*, "The results should be taught in medical school and driven home by health insurance companies and posted on the bulletin boards of every nursing home in the country, where nearly a fifth of the residents have depression."

Unfortunately, that's not how it works in the United States.

The US medical system might have some built-in barriers to exercise being viewed as a viable, stand-alone treatment. It remains the case that physicians are trained more to deal with disease than to promote health. We go to a doctor's office not to learn how to live life to its fullest, but because something is wrong with us. We go with the expectation that the doctor has something to offer—a prescription, a test or two, a referral to a specialist—above and beyond what we can do on our own. Understandably, most doctors probably feel that they should offer something reflecting their education and experience. The doctor saying, "Try getting outside and moving your body for half an hour most days, then come see me in six weeks" isn't how a typical office visit plays out for either party. The more cynical among us might also mention how pharmaceutical companies promote the idea that there's a pill to pop for most maladies.

Current guidelines by groups such as the American Psychiatric Association and the American College of Physicians don't count exercise as what's known as a first-line treatment, or an initial form of treatment a physician should recommend for a patient with depression. (Modern antidepressants and some forms of psychotherapy are the two main first-line treatments.) On a patient portion of its website, the National Institute of Mental Health includes exercise in a section called "Beyond Treatment: Things You Can Do" along with things like "set realistic goals for yourself" and "continue to educate yourself about depression."

In contrast, guidelines in countries such as the United Kingdom, the Netherlands, and Canada recommend that clinicians view exercise as a first-line treatment. Canada, for example, recommends exercise as an initial stand-alone treatment for mild to moderate depression and a second-line, or next-round, treatment in conjunction with other treatments for more severe cases. Guidelines in Australia and New Zealand view exercise even more favorably. Incorporating the evidence for inactivity contributing to depression, the Royal Australian and New Zealand College of Psychiatrists guidelines consider exercise a "step-zero" treatment. That is, a sedentary depressed patient in Sydney or Auckland will first be encouraged to start working out. Only if regular exercise proves to be insufficient will the US go-tos of medication and psychotherapy be tried.

Back in the US, exercise as medicine might be an instance in which patients lead and standard practice catches up. Ideally, more physicians and clinicians will hear from the people they treat how running and other forms of exercise help them manage depression. Here's one such story.

BECOMING DEPRESSED, BECOMING A RUNNER

Unlike many with the condition, I've never been majorly incapacitated by depression. Most people would consider me productive, accomplished, perhaps even energetic, given that my lifetime running odometer is past 110,000 miles. I have dysthymia—chronic, low-grade depression. The literal translation is "ill-humored." I liken dysthymia to the rusty-coil sensation I deal with where my left hamstring attaches to the pelvis—it's been with me for decades, it's almost never bad enough to merit time off, but it's always there in the background, and if I'm not diligent about self-care, it goes from manageable to miserable.

Like the hamstring-insertion discomfort, my dysthymia and I have been together a long time. I was always a "moody" kid. When I'd go into one of what she called my funks, my mother would ask, "What's wrong?" "I don't know, I just feel sad," I'd answer, which usually produced the response, "Well, snap out of it." Nothing horrible ever happened. I was never abused, we weren't destitute, no one close to me died, I had friends and siblings to do things with, I was good at school. But nothing special ever happened, either. Two p.m. on a gray March Tuesday is my image of childhood.

The current me in my mind's eye started to crystallize in ninth grade. A few key things happened that school year: I became more goal-oriented, I got ruminatively depressed, and I started running. That they all happened at roughly the same time isn't a coincidence.

One day in biology class, the topic was freshwater ecosystems. Among the creatures we learned about was the mayfly. The species in our reading was one in which the adult stage lasts twenty-four hours. Nymphs emerge from water as adults, mate, and die within the space of a day. Adults don't have the capacity to eat, because they don't need to.

I was barely able to do my homework that night. The life cycle of the mayfly saddened me in a way that nothing had before. What was the point, I wondered, of being born only to live long enough to produce the next generation of similarly doomed mayflies? Why couldn't the mayflies live for forty-eight hours, so that they could have a day to enjoy themselves before mating and dying? It then struck me that the two-day existence didn't really have much more meaning, nor three, nor four, nor . . .

I had long observed my family, wondering why we did what we did, especially on weekends when the usual routines of school and work were absent. How did we choose to spend our time? Often it seemed we were doing things simply to fill the hours between meals, and soon enough the weekend would be over and we'd be back to not having to think of things to do. And what was the point of that, I wondered, any more than the mayfly and its sad twenty-four-hour life cycle?

Years later I learned the word *weltschmerz*. Its literal translation from the German is "world (*Welt*) pain (*Schmerz*)." It refers to sadness over the gap between how you'd like the world to be and reality. If I'd known it in ninth grade I would have gone to school the next day with a note reading, "Please excuse Scott's mood. He's experiencing mayfly-induced weltschmerz." Pangs of disappointment over the underlying unsatisfactory nature of life have been with me ever since. ("Patients with an intellectual inclination may belabor themes of alienation and the absurdities of the human condition," the book *Dysthymia and the Spectrum of Chronic Depressions* warns therapists.)

Around this time I began to set ambitious goals. Instead of being a good student, I'd get straight A's. Instead of almost always going to school, I'd have perfect attendance. Instead of schlepping along in Boy Scouts because I liked camping,

I'd become an Eagle Scout. Without understanding it at the time, I now realize I did this because of the burgeoning dysthymia. My version of depression's second main feature is anhedonia—a diminished ability to experience pleasure. These goals were ways to feel more engaged with what I'd be doing anyway. It wasn't as if there were tons of enjoyable activities that school and other forms of hurdle-hopping were keeping me from. So, why not set the hurdles a little higher to better occupy myself?

It was also around this time that I first got drunk, smoked pot, and had a girlfriend. Now here were things that addressed anhedonia and weltschmerz! With concentrated listening, the right music could also bring great pleasure by taking me somewhere I wasn't being dragged down by the usual we're-all-mayflies thoughts.

Running was the other big novelty of those days. I'd had small tastes of it in gym class, where one option during the track-and-field unit was to jog the perimeter of the school grounds rather than long jump or sprint. Doing so was enjoyable. As it happened, one of my sisters had a friend who had been the state cross-country champion. He had run the local Jaycees' Walk for Humanity twenty-mile fund-raiser; that impressed me more than his state championship. The idea of being so capable and independent was captivating. Throughout my childhood I'd often felt that I wanted to be doing something different, but I didn't know what it was. Now I did. High school and organized competition didn't start until tenth grade, but I knew I was going to go out for the cross-country team, so I started running on March 1, 1979, in the spring of ninth grade.

I was soon doing ten- and twelve-milers, and sometimes running twice a day. Like my teen forays into sex, drugs, and rock and roll, running countered anhedonia and weltschmerz. It was invigorating mentally and physically while I did it, and in the afterglow I was briefly freed from yearning for a better elsewhere. Running also gave structure to the day and imparted meaning to otherwise banal matters, such as what and when to eat. Even my mother, who was not elated that her teen son disappeared to who-knows-where an hour or two a day and had become really skinny, appreciated running's mental-health effects. When my aura of sourness became too overwhelming, she'd say, "Why don't you go for a run?"

When I got to high school and started training with the team, running became even more key to my well-being. Two of the guys I ran thousands of miles with back then remain close friends. At road races I became friendly with adult runners, who gave me hope that running could be part of my long-term future. Running became a dependable source of pleasure and relief that, partly by providing structure to my days, always provided something to look forward to. I knew I'd finally found a way to make life more livable, run by run, day by day.

What I didn't know was that I was changing the very structure of my brain.

BUILDING A BETTER BRAIN

In my early days of running, I discovered (and reveled in) its effects on my mood. It was amazing to leave the house and return just thirty minutes later feeling more energetic, optimistic, engaged, and happy. And doing so didn't require talking my brother into buying me beer! That immediate and dependable boost in mood is one of running's great attractions, regardless of your mental health. Short-term relief is especially captivating for runners with depression. In chapter 4, we'll look in detail at why any given run makes you feel so much better, and how best to get that benefit.

But where running really helps with depression is over time, thanks to changes in brain structure. According to Panteleimon Ekkekakis, PhD, a researcher and professor of exercise psychology at Iowa State University, regular running produces the same two changes that are thought to be responsible for the effectiveness of modern antidepressants: increased levels of the neurotransmitters serotonin and norepinephrine, and neurogenesis—the creation of new brain cells. As Laura Fredendall says, "The daily hits matter, but over time there's a cumulative effect. You're actually building a healthier brain, and a healthier brain's going to feel better."

Much of this change happens in the hippocampus, an area of the brain that's often shrunken in people with depression. According to Ekkekakis, "MRI scans have shown that even after a six-month exercise intervention, there's a visible increase in the size of the hippocampus." (Reinforcing the uncertainty about the causes of depression, Ekkekakis says, "The hippocampus is primarily involved in memory. We don't understand why growth in an area of the brain that appears to be involved with memory would somehow contribute to an antidepressant effect, but there seems to be a link.")

That regular running causes structural changes in the brain is the most important thing I learned writing this book. It makes sense once you think about it: Why wouldn't there be noticeable differences over time in the brain, in the same way that a chest X-ray shows that the left ventricle of my heart has enlarged over decades of running? But growing the brain by running isn't something you often hear about. Discussions of its mental-health benefits tend to focus on day-to-day effects, implying that using running to manage depression is a Sisyphean task that starts from scratch with each sunrise. Research says otherwise: Running produces neurogenesis and neuroplasticity (improvements in the brain's internal communications network).[8]

Neurogenesis and neuroplasticity appear to occur primarily due to brain-derived neurotrophic factor, the protein briefly discussed in the previous chapter. (*Trophic*, in this context, means promoting survival and growth of the brain cells known as neurons.) Brain-derived neurotrophic factor (BDNF) is often called the Miracle-Gro of the brain. "It helps neurons fire and wire together," Fredendall says. The hippocampus, with its mysterious link to depression, is a key area of BDNF activity. Increased levels of BDNF appear to encourage both new growth and better functioning of existing neurons that are involved in serotonergic transmission. Again, this mechanism of increasing the availability of neurotransmitters, such as serotonin, is exactly what modern antidepressants aim to achieve.

BDNF levels sharply increase after any given workout.[9] Or more accurately, any aerobic workout, such as running. Most research hasn't found that such activities as strength training boost BDNF levels.[10] This acute increase in BDNF levels during a run is part of why you can almost guarantee you'll return from a run in a better mood. But where we runners really get help is over time. People who exercise regularly have greater BDNF increases per workout than less committed exercisers. For each run, you get more of the good stuff. Your other reward for regularity: There's research indicating that frequent exercisers have higher BDNF levels at rest than do sedentary people.[11] So, even when you're not running, the fact that you do so regularly is bettering your brain.

Of course, you probably don't possess charts of your typical BDNF levels before and since you became a runner. What you do have are your subjective experiences. Reflecting on them might help you realize that more time as a runner can mean less interference from depression.

"Neurogenesis from running also occurs in the prefrontal cortex," Fredendall says. "That's a superimportant part of the brain. People who are stress-resilient show more activity in the left side of the prefrontal cortex. Running and doing other hard things, where you push yourself, increases activity in the prefrontal cortex. Over time, that builds a brain that's better able to regulate itself." Or, as a review of research published in *Clinical Psychology Review* put it, "exercise training recruits a process which confers enduring resilience to stress."[12]

There's another key physiological way that running helps depression. It occurs by the seeming paradox of expending energy to feel more energetic.

ACTIVATION SAVES THE DAY

I once explained the lethargy of depression to my brother by asking him what he does when he's thirsty. He gave me a "Duh" look and said, "Get something to drink." I said it's not always that simple. I told him I might feel thirsty and think, "I should go to the kitchen and get some water." Then, I might imagine rising from a chair, walking to another room, getting a glass, and turning on the faucet. Often, I said, picturing myself going through that process leads to the thought, "That's a lot of work. Stay put until you're ready."

This prehearsal of desired activities before deciding not to do them sounds strange to people like my brother, but brings nods of understanding from people with depression. Fatigue is often listed as a symptom of depression. I don't think that's quite the right word. Fatigue is being seventeen miles into a hilly twenty-miler when your longest run in the last two months was fourteen miles. "Perceived fatigue" more accurately captures the phenomenon of thinking about doing something and postponing doing it until you feel you have enough energy. Initiative can be especially lacking if your depression includes a feeling of meaninglessness. Why bother getting up and doing something if your efforts don't matter? Inertia can take on a life of its own; a body at rest tends to stay at rest, after all, which leads to feeling that much droopier.

Running is a daily way to break free from lassitude. Getting out the door changes the narrative and creates momentum. "I think of running as helping depression through activation, through the improved energy that comes from running," says clinical psychiatrist Brian Vasey. Fredendall says of people with depression, "I have not had a patient who wouldn't benefit from increasing their activity level. When you're depressed, your brain is more turned off. Going for a run activates your brain cells. Having that wake-up experience can make you feel better."

In my early years of running, I often struggled with activation. I'd picture myself five miles from home and think, "Not yet. Wait until you're up for it." This happened even though I knew that the magical infusion of energy I was waiting for would come only by doing the thing I was finding reasons to avoid. I seldom have these silly procrastination battles now. I have decades more evidence that just a few miles will energize mind and body like nothing else.

Another key is internalizing the lesson that something is better than nothing in these situations. That's another way of saying when you know you need a run, don't visualize yourself five miles from home. On my worst days with depression, I tell myself all that's required is a token run, at no faster than a stumble. If you feel worse after ten minutes, the internal monologue goes, you can go home. You can probably guess that I almost always stay out longer, and return home feeling victorious.

To bridge the gap between hibernating sloth and runner in motion, I picture myself going to bed that night. As I turn off the light, will I be happier that I got myself to run? Of course. I also find a way to change into my running clothes and start my prerun routine of stretching and other exercises. On particularly tough days, I tell myself all I have to do in the immediate future is some gentle stretching, which will feel better if I'm wearing running gear. This low level of activity starts the energizing process; seeing myself outside and in motion begins to seem possible. Fredendall will sometimes have a patient stand and join her in breathing exercises or arm swings to get a slight activation effect.

Rich Harfst has also learned over the years that running can be most helpful when it seems least likely. After competing in high school and college, he was a self-described fitness runner for the first part of his professional life. When he began to run again after back surgery in 2004, he decided to resume racing, and now, in his fifties, is trying to break 3:00 for the marathon.

"I've achieved a point—knock on wood—where I'm pretty good at heading it off," Harfst says of days-long depressive episodes that used to be more common. "The worst periods are now down to a matter of days, where I just fight my way out of it. That's where running comes in—I stay consistent even on really bad days. Something might happen and I might crawl in a hole and go to bed for a while, but I'll get out of bed and go for a run just because I don't want to put a zero in my training log. It slowly starts to bring me out on the other side."

The just-do-it approach isn't to belittle the struggles of runners who sometimes miss days even though they know running will energize them. Rob Krar is a two-time winner of the Western States Endurance Run, a hundred-miler that's considered the most prestigious ultramarathon in the United States. Yet even he sometimes finds himself dressed to run and simply unable to step through the door to a better day. "I don't have that magic wand to wave and get myself out of it," the Flagstaff, Arizona, resident says. "Sometimes I can and sometimes I can't."

Ian Kellogg is another fast runner whose competitive goals aren't enough to activate him when his depression is especially bad. "More often than not, I don't run on those days, even though I know that just half an hour will make me feel better," the Otterbein University cross-country ace says. "I can't find the energy or willpower to get out the door."

Kellogg's father, John, is also a runner. He's often Ian's escort out of the negative feedback loop of inactivity. "My dad will say, 'Come jog a few miles with me,'" Ian says. "He understands what's going on in my head. My best memories are going on runs with my dad and talking or sometimes not talking at all. If he does that a few times, that helps me get out of my funk, or it at least sparks a drive for me to get running again. And then I'm usually able to get back to normal."

Conventional wisdom advises arranging runs with others for people who lack consistency, on the theory that you're less likely to blow off a run if you know someone is waiting for you. Fredendall would approve of the elder Kellogg's wiliness in applying this advice to his son's depression. "If you're depressed, you might be more likely to show up for someone else than you are to show up for yourself," she says. Tricking yourself in this way means activation, and the relief from depressive symptoms that comes with it. It can also lead to a feeling of self-efficacy, another key way in which running helps people with depression.

SPREADING SELF-EFFICACY

The short- and long-term effects of running on your brain and body are profound. But levels of chemicals in your brain are only part of your mental state. There's also cognition—mental processes. Cognition includes not just straightforward thinking ("I should run long today because a blizzard is coming tomorrow") but also more involved phenomena, such as how you think about your thoughts.

A hallmark of depression is self-defeating, absolutist thinking: "Everything is harder than it should be." "There's no pleasure in my life." "It doesn't matter what I do." "It's always going to be like this." Running gives us regular opportunities to prove those thoughts wrong and thereby feel better, and feel better about ourselves. "For people with depression, a big psychological benefit from running is a boost in self-esteem," Vasey says. "Having been able to set a goal and reach it brings confidence." As Amelia Gapin, from New Jersey, says, "If I knock out ten miles before work I feel like I'm on a high the rest of the day."

Fredendall agrees that this psychological benefit of running is key: "The subjective experience of seeing yourself do something can make you feel better. Success in doing the hard thing and being in a running program gives people a sense of self-efficacy—the prediction or belief in one's ability to be able to perform or accomplish a specific task or goal. That really helps with mood management for a lot of people."

Over time, the self-efficacy aspect of running has become one of the sport's main aids to my life. I've learned that lacing up and hitting the roads is my best way to break free from "What's the point?" on autorepeat. On a daily basis, running reminds me that I can overcome apathy and torpor. Seeing that small victory, I can convince myself that progress is possible in meeting professional goals, or not feeling lonely so often, or figuring out how to afford retirement, or improving my posture.

Ekkekakis is also big on the benefits of self-efficacy. It's one reason that he wishes exercise were prescribed at least as often as antidepressants.

"If you take antidepressants and they make you better, the psychological attribution is external," he says. "Patients believe that the reason they get better is because of the drug they take. People believe, 'I cannot even function without having to rely on this external thing that helps me get through the day.'

"With exercise," he says, "the attribution is internal: 'The reason I get better is because I myself try. It's not that somebody else is giving me a pill, it's that I am putting in the effort.' That's where perhaps the additional benefit of exercise compared to the antidepressants lies—that sense of empowerment, that sense that I myself am taking control of my situation."

"Taking control of my situation" is an apt description of how running has helped me manage depression. It applies at least equally as well to how running helps people with anxiety, which is the subject of the next chapter.

CHAPTER 3

How Running Helps People with Anxiety

On a long run one spring morning, a friend said she was worried about her daughter's upcoming trip to Paris. There had been a terrorist attack in the city a couple of months earlier, and my friend was worried about a repeat. I unhelpfully trotted out the usual question: "Do you worry this much every time she gets in a car? She's a lot more likely to die that way."

The odds of dying in a terrorist attack segued into the friend voicing her fear of death. (Love that runner's high!) I continued in the hyper-rational devil's advocate role. What exactly are you afraid of? I asked. If the worst thing that can happen in any situation is that you die, then in the situation when you do die, the worst has happened, so there's nothing to fear. Even if it's really painful, it will soon be over, and then you won't have to live with the consequences and memory of that pain. My friend said it was the fear of the unknown that troubled her—what it's like while it's happening and what happens after. I said I'm all for worrying about known upcoming events that you can make better by prepping for; what's known as defensive pessimism is my forte. But worrying about unknowns that you have no way of learning more about and that you can do nothing to change? That just makes no sense, I said.

This was not my best moment as empathetic running partner. As someone whose depressive thoughts often lack logic, I should have understood it's immaterial whether my friend's anxiety about death withstands rational analysis. That's especially true because I know that one of the main reasons my friend runs is to manage anxiety.

Much of what we learned above about how running helps people with depression is also true for people with anxiety. But anxiety presents its own challenges. In this chapter we'll look at the many ways that running is highly effective in addressing those challenges.

A QUICK OVERVIEW OF ANXIETY

As with occasionally feeling sad and having depression, it helps to distinguish worrying about things from what medically is known as anxiety disorder. The worry that underlies anxiety disorder is often nebulous, as opposed to, say, worrying about work. "I talk about anxiety as agitated, uncomfortable, something not right with the world, stress that could be a feeling of threat or a feeling of worry, a feeling of discomfort that often leads to seeking out relief through different means, sometimes unhealthy means," says clinical psychiatrist Brian Vasey. These thoughts and sensations are often accompanied by physical symptoms associated with the body's fight-or-flight mechanism, such as increased heart rate and sweating.

One factor is persistence, and subsequent interference with day-to-day functioning. "If someone said, 'I have these symptoms but they don't really bother me, I don't have daily physical symptoms that are distracting, I'm not spending a lot of time engaged in coping,' I wouldn't diagnose that person as having an anxiety disorder," Vasey says.

Clinically, anxiety has different categories, including general anxiety disorder, social anxiety disorder, and panic disorder. It's estimated that almost 29 percent of Americans will develop an anxiety disorder at some point in their life.[1] Clinical social worker Frank Brooks says that about 20 percent of the population will have anxiety in a given year, underlying its chronic nature. Adding to the toll of anxiety is that it's often accompanied by depression. "I more often find that anxiety and depression coexist rather than being two separate entities, with the depression frequently a result of untreated anxiety over time," Vasey says. Estimates of anxiety's and depression's coexistence range from 50 to 80 percent.

As shown by my on-the-run cluelessness discussing my friend's fear of death, I'm one of the fortunate people with

depression who don't have anxiety. To get a better understanding, I asked several people who use running to manage
their anxiety to describe their symptoms.

Cecilia Bidwell, an attorney from Tampa, Florida, didn't
experience anxiety until her midtwenties, when she was in
law school. "I started having these days where I was gripped
by feelings of dread and terrible worry," she says. "It would
always be about something specific—like a guy I was seeing
at the time who's now my husband was deployed in Iraq, and
I'd wake up some days convinced he was going to be killed.
Or I'd wake up absolutely convinced I would never pass the
background check to be admitted to the bar and wouldn't
be able to practice law."

When she began practicing, the incidents became more
frequent, and less tied to specific incidents. Once she was driving back from a meeting and had to pull off I-95 into a Whole
Foods Market parking lot: "I couldn't breathe, my heart was
racing, I felt like my chest was being crushed in. I thought I'd
developed cardiomyopathy from running ultramarathons."
Before she learned how to manage her anxiety with running
and other measures of self-care, she struggled to maintain the
composure and air of confidence expected of a trial attorney. "I
think I did come across as something of a complete mess," she
says. "I once got a less-than-favorable end-of-year evaluation
where I was told, 'You have all this nervous energy,' and I was
thinking, 'You have no freakin' idea.'"

Heather Johnson's anxiety began at age thirteen. The
South Portland, Maine, resident was on a plane that was

delayed for hours because of a snowstorm. That triggered her first panic attack. "I was so scared, and I couldn't understand what was happening inside my body," she says. "I stood up and slapped my own face, because that's what they do in the movies to bring someone back to reality." Johnson walked off the flight and couldn't be talked back on. "I had a few more of these types of situations, and then I started to fear the fear of these situations."

Johnson, who is one of my running partners, had many physical symptoms when she was young, including racing heart, sweating hands, shakiness, weakness in the knees, and dizziness. "Diarrhea was a big one for me," she says, "and I had an immense fear of going [to the bathroom] in public, which meant if this symptom popped up at any time, I panicked even more until I got home." In her midforties, Johnson has far fewer physical manifestations. "Now I experience racing thoughts, rumination, an insatiable need to know everything that is dangerous and how to avoid it, cure it, or what will happen if I or someone I know gets it," she says. "I still have some specific phobias, but I've learned to manage them so they don't keep me at home."

Ian Kellogg, the Otterbein University student-athlete, has also dealt with anxiety since childhood. "One way it's always shown up is that I'm a chronic overthinker," he says. "I'm really physically and emotionally sensitive about things. When I was really young I would only wear specific outfits because of how they fit on my body. The night before the first day of fifth grade, I had a breakdown and told my parents I didn't want to go to school any more, even though there was absolutely no reason why."

Another of my running partners, Meredith Anderson, whom we met in the introduction, experiences anxiety primarily as dread of the coming day, either the night before or in the morning. "It's about both specific things and tomorrow as a concept," she says. "There are thoughts of, 'You're going to fail,' 'It's not going to go well,' 'You're not good enough.' And then it can be difficult to stop those negative thoughts having to do with self-esteem." Anderson deals with the dread by eating more than she thinks she should and by delaying going to bed: "I stay up because then the next day doesn't come sooner."

When the next day does come, Anderson handles it best by starting it with a run. There's good evidence backing that choice.

THE CASE FOR RUNNING AS A TREATMENT FOR ANXIETY

Despite anxiety being more prevalent than depression, there have been fewer studies conducted on whether exercise is an effective treatment. A partial explanation has to do with the nature of research and anxiety. Peer-reviewed studies try to have strictly defined parameters. Whereas depression is typically seen as symptoms along a single spectrum, anxiety is more heterogeneous, making it more difficult to conform to a standard research model.

What the research that has been done shows is that aerobic exercise, such as running, has what the experts call an anxiolytic effect, meaning that it reduces symptoms of anxiety. Workouts longer than thirty minutes are generally found to provide more benefit, and, as with most things related to running, consistency is king.

Evidence from studies such as ones on more than 8,000 Americans and 19,000 Dutch regularly shows that regular exercisers are at less risk of being diagnosed with anxiety.[2] Of course, these findings offer the possibility that people with anxiety might be less likely to work out regularly.

If we turn instead to studies on people diagnosed with anxiety who begin working out, the findings are similarly pro-exercise. Almost three decades ago, a review of research on the topic stated, "The results substantiate the claim that exercise is associated with reductions in anxiety, but only for aerobic forms of exercise."[3] As more studies have been conducted, regular aerobic exercise has consistently been shown to reduce anxiety symptoms compared to placebo or no treatment. This is true even when people with a chronic illness, such as heart disease or cancer, begin exercising. A 2010 review of research on such patients found that those who worked out regularly reported an average 20 percent reduction in their anxiety symptoms.[4] As a 2017 review of the most up-to-date research concluded, "Taken together with the wider benefits of exercise on wellbeing and cardiovascular health, these findings reinforce exercise as an important treatment option in people with anxiety/stress disorders."[5]

Because of fewer studies on exercise and anxiety compared to exercise and depression, there's not as much data on exercise's effectiveness compared to other common forms of treatment. Still, a 2015 review of research stated: "The majority of studies concluded that, as a treatment for elevated anxiety or anxiety disorders, exercise offers benefits comparable to established treatments, including medication or [cognitive behavioral therapy], and better than those of placebo or waitlist control [people in a study who are told they're on a waiting list to receive the study's active treatment]."[6] The same review concluded that there are too few studies on the topic to conclude whether exercise in addition to another form of treatment is more effective than either treatment by itself.

One key takeaway from these research reviews is that exercise such as running helps with both state anxiety and trait anxiety. State anxiety is a temporary manifestation of anxiety symptoms in response to a specific situation. For example, you might feel trapped upon entering a loud, crowded room, and react psychologically and physically. When the specific situation no longer presents itself—in this case, when you leave the room—your symptoms go away.

Trait anxiety is a more permanent aspect of personality, a tendency to regularly experience the symptoms of anxiety. You might have those symptoms to a higher degree than most people, or you might experience symptoms more often, or both. The research on exercise and trait anxiety shows significant help only with regularity. The 1991 review found that symptoms of trait anxiety didn't improve significantly until after ten or more weeks of regular workouts.

How do running and other forms of regular aerobic exercise produce these profound benefits? As with running and depression, there are thought to be several key means that work together to make exercise medicinal.

A MORE PEACEFUL COEXISTENCE

Remember that anxiety and depression often coexist. People with anxiety often receive prescriptions for two types of modern antidepressants: selective serotonin reuptake inhibitors (SSRIs) and serotonin-norepinephrine reuptake inhibitors (SNRIs). The two conditions' coexistence and presumed similar underlying agency also mean that the brain changes caused by running that we looked at in the previous chapter—increased levels of brain-derived neurotropic factor (BDNF) and growth in the hippocampus—apply to people with anxiety as well as depression.

In this view, running helps people with anxiety not just because any one workout improves their mood. Regular running helps create new brain cells and foster better communication within the brain, a structural change that helps to lessen anxiety. This idea meshes well with the finding that most people experience significant reduction in their anxiety symptoms only after several weeks of regular exercise.

An animal study suggests another structural change that might help with anxiety.[7] Researchers at Princeton University gave one group of mice unlimited access to a running wheel, while keeping another group sedentary. (Mice in these situations generally run voluntarily. What else do they have to do?) After six weeks of this setup, all the mice were briefly exposed to cold water. The researchers looked at activity in the mice's ventral hippocampus (an area of the brain that regulates anxiety) resulting from that stress.

In the sedentary mice, genes in hippocampal neurons associated with stress reactions began turning on almost immediately. That didn't happen with the running mice. That was the case even though the running mice had, via exercise, generated new neurons, which are usually more excitable than older neurons. Instead, the brains of the running mice showed an increase in activities that inhibit stressful reactions, including releasing large amounts of the neurotransmitter gamma-aminobutyric acid. This neurotransmitter, known popularly as GABA, plays a major role in reducing brain cell excitability, thus providing a calming effect. (Perhaps predictably, GABA supplements are sold as a stress reliever.)

All indications are that running gave these mice a better ability to manage stress. Findings such as these, Iowa State professor Panteleimon Ekkekakis says, suggest "that the [anxiety-reducing] effect of exercise is not merely cognitive." After all, the running mice presumably didn't fare better when exposed to the stress of cold water by telling themselves, "You can handle this—it can't be any worse than that long run in the wheel last week."

That's not to downplay the cognitive aspect of running for us humans. The psychological benefits that help people with depression accrue at least as significantly for those with anxiety. Heather Johnson's experiences sync perfectly with the findings of a Southern Methodist University study.[8] It tested whether regular exposure to exercise helps with what's known as anxiety sensitivity, which is interpreting anxiety-related sensations, such as increased heart rate and respiration, as signs of impending disaster. The participants in the study had the same success as Johnson, who says, "Running has been instrumental in pushing me into situations that trigger the same symptoms as a panic attack. It gives me ample opportunity to employ the skills necessary to abate negative self-talk, confront the fear of body symptoms (racing heart, feelings of fatigue, etc.), and enjoy the moment."

Johnson is also an example of increased self-efficacy via running. Formerly fearful in crowds to the point of incapacitation, she now regularly runs large road races, in all their jam-packed starting corral glory. She has also managed the marketing department of a large communications firm and served on the local school board. "Every time I push outside of my comfort zone—whether running a new route and resisting the temptation to turn earlier in the run to avoid running too far away from home, or running a race and getting through the postrace fatigue—is an achievement," she says.

SOOTHING STRIDES

For people with depression, a benefit of running is the seeming paradox of activation—getting up and moving makes
you more energetic rather than more tired. For anxiety,
running also has a potentially counterintuitive benefit: An
activity that raises your heart rate and blood pressure and per-
spiration, which are common physical symptoms of anxiety,
can be calming. Anderson says about a good prework run,
"Whatever's going on in the day, I'm going to have a feeling
like I can handle it."

Ekkekakis says he's unaware of specific research on the
brain mechanism behind the tranquilizing effect of exercise. "We do know, however, that exercise simulates some of
the peripheral effects of tranquilizers, inducing reductions
in [muscle activity] typically associated with tension and
anxiety." He notes that, after a run, there's a drop in blood
pressure, and your heart rate and systolic blood pressure don't
increase in response to typical emotional stressors in the way
that they do when you haven't just worked out.

J. Carson Smith, the University of Maryland brain
researcher we met in chapter 1, has done some interesting
work on the calming effects of exercise. In one study, he
found that people were more drawn to images of pleasant
faces when working out at moderate intensity than they were
at rest.[9] Smith measured this change with what's known as a
dot-probe task. The subjects in the study stared at a cross in
the center of a computer screen designed to fix their attention. Pairs of faces—one face neutral, one either pleasant or

unpleasant—appeared on each side of the center of the screen for one second. Then a dot appeared where one of the faces had been. The subjects were asked to locate where the dot appeared as quickly and accurately as possible.

The dot-probe task is a standard test for attentional bias, or paying attention to some things at the expense of others. Smith found that when the subjects were working out at a moderate intensity, they paid significantly more attention to the pleasant faces; they were more likely to accurately locate where those images had appeared on screen. Meanwhile, their attentional bias to the unpleasant faces decreased; they simply didn't notice these images as often. The subjects showed no such bias toward the pleasant faces or away from the unpleasant faces when they did the test at rest or while working out at high intensity.

In another study, Smith measured people's anxiety levels on two occasions, before and after they sat peacefully for thirty minutes, and before and after they worked out at a moderate intensity for half an hour.[10] The subjects were less anxious after both the chill-out sitting and exercise. Then came the twist. Fifteen minutes later, after both conditions, the subjects looked at ninety pictures on a computer screen. Thirty were classified as neutral (people, places, and objects); thirty were deemed pleasant (fifteen of babies, families, and cute animals, fifteen of erotica); and thirty were unpleasant (depicting threat and mutilation).

When the people looked at these images after their half-hour sit, their anxiety levels returned to what they'd been at the beginning of the session. But when they looked at the images fifteen minutes after exercising, their anxiety levels remained lower. Having recently finished a workout appeared to give them a bulwark against emotional manipulation.

Bidwell finds that a prolonged postrun calm carries through her stressful work days. "It's kind of a reset," she says about running in the morning. "If I've gone for a good run in the morning, I'm fine at two p.m. if things are going haywire. I'm handling them a lot better, I'm less worried about them, I'm not heading into crises about 'why am I here?' If I'm feeling anxious and worried about stuff and go for a run, it fixes that, but it's also more useful as a preventative everyday thing."

THINK DIFFERENT

When people talk about clearing their mind with a good run, they can mean getting rid of thoughts that have bedraggled them for the last however many hours. That can happen both because of distraction ("gosh, look at the pretty flowers") or focus ("the most important thing in the world right now is that I run this fifth eight-hundred-meter repeat as fast as the first four"). Meredith Anderson says, "More often than not, when I come back from a run by myself whatever thoughts were nagging me aren't there anymore, and I didn't do a ton of work to get there. It's not like I was doing a lot of cognitive behavioral therapy and challenging those negative thoughts. It was the running that made the difference." Heather Johnson says only running "produces a zone-out effect, kind of like when you're driving and ten minutes pass, but you don't remember it."

But clearing the mind can also come not so much from erasing previous thoughts as from getting clarity on them. This mobile magic was consistently cited as a main appeal of running when I talked to people with anxiety. Cecilia Bidwell puts it this way: "When I'm running, the thoughts come in and out, and I'm not worried. I can think about things objectively. Things that I'm thinking are a huge deal I realize aren't a big deal in the scheme of things." Johnson says, "Running is the best cure for the swirling thought-storm in my head. I can literally start a run where my head is buzzing the entire time, bouncing from one thought, problem, conversation, to the other, but by the end, it disappears. It's how I resolve my internal conflicts or work out problems."

Clinical psychologist Laura Fredendall agrees that running is a great escape from rumination: "When we're overwhelmed with anxiety and depression, shifting from the big picture—all the frustrations, worst-case scenario thinking— to the small, in-the-moment task of doing something that approaches a goal, like running a four-mile loop with two hills, will kick off a positive feedback loop that continues throughout the run and takes our thinking and emotions out of the trench of negativity."

Ekkekakis believes the think-different benefit of running is likely a combination of two factors. "On the one hand, neurotransmitters that promote a pleasurable sensation and help you put a positive spin on things," he says, citing endo-cannabinoids, which have a similar chemical structure to the active ingredient in marijuana (and which we'll look at in depth in the next chapter). "Second, the [circulatory system] changes that happen with moderate exercise." In particular, it's probable that more oxygenated blood going to the prefrontal cortex of the brain is key. The prefrontal cortex helps with rational thinking. Greater activity there should logically lead to the clarity on otherwise troublesome topics that Bidwell and others regularly experience while running.

ANXIETY ABOUT THE THING THAT USUALLY HELPS WITH YOUR ANXIETY

Most of the people I talked with about this topic said that running is a respite from anxiety. Bidwell, for example, says, "Most of my friends who are less anxious than me usually are far more anxious about their race times than I am. If a workout doesn't go well or I have to cut a run short, I'm like, 'It is what it is.'" But not everyone is able to be so nonchalant.

"There's a really, really fine line for me leading up to a big race with managing my anxiety," Ian Kellogg says. "Am I going to approach this race with a positive, intentional attitude, or am I going to let it control me from two weeks out? There have been times when I've let it control everything that's going on in my mind. I have trouble focusing in school, trouble going to bed, things like that, because I'm constantly anxious or waiting around for this one event."

Anderson says, "Anxiety was the main reason for me not running well in high school and college. I know that most people get nervous before races. But with the nervousness came the negative thoughts, like 'It's not going to go well.'" Her dread of the race would build in the few days before, peaking as she was standing on the start line. During races, she says, "the negative thoughts would come when I got tired. That's when things could really turn—negative thoughts then were harder to come back from."

Kellogg says that not managing anxiety cost him a chance at a school record. At an indoor meet, he was in the fast heat of the mile; the race would almost certainly be won faster than Otterbein's record of 4:14.5. The pack went through the first four hundred meters in sixty-five seconds, a little slower than Kellogg's goal pace. "Instead of understanding it would wind up and people would soon start to go faster, I panicked," he says. "I told myself I'm not a good kicker. I surged to the front and hammered the middle eight hundred meters and then fell apart the last four hundred." The race wound up being won in the time Kellogg wanted to run. He was six seconds back, in 4:20.

I was surprised to hear Anderson's stories of prerace dread. Now in her late thirties, she's one of the most enthusiastic road racers I've ever met. The difference, she says, is that she's now running and racing solely for herself. "In school, there was some kind of pressure that I put on myself because of being on a team—that I had to do well and I couldn't mess up, and what would people think if I did, which became a self-fulfilling prophecy."

Kellogg has learned to better manage running-related anxiety by changing his prerace routine. "I used to put headphones on and get super hyped-up, but that causes me to psych myself out and overthink the race," he says. Now, he tries to stay as calm as possible by joking around with his teammates.

He continues, "I still get very nervous before races, but when I'm standing on the starting line, there's no place in the world I'd rather be. Having those thoughts before my races is extremely important for me—they remind me that I'm ready to go and that I enjoy what I'm doing.

"Aside from racing, I've learned to really enjoy the act of just going for a run," Kellogg says. "While there's nothing better than nailing a good workout or smashing a PR, there's something therapeutic about going for an easy ten-miler."

Just why do Kellogg and the rest of us find an easy ten-miler so therapeutic, such a pleasurable interlude from the demands of the workaday world? Running's effects on our short-term emotional state, or mood, is our next topic.

CHAPTER 4

How to Use Running to Improve Your Mood

Sunday, February 12, may have been the most unusual day of 2017 for me.

I ran for seventy minutes—nothing out of the ordinary there. The logistics of the run were also typical for winter in Maine: I had Stabilicers on my shoes because of the previous day's as well as currently falling snow, and I did short loops of a nearby neighborhood that gets slightly better plowing. Even my falling a few times didn't really distinguish the run.

What made the day unique was that I returned from the run in a worse mood. ("This absolutely sucked," my running log entry begins.) Heavier snow was forecast for the next few days, so I'd wanted to get in something other than a token run. More important, decades of doing so had taught me that, even on runs that were drudgery, my mood would improve if

I stayed out long enough. But not this day. As I flailed around Ferry Village, it felt as if every driver who passed me was more likely than the last to get flipped off, every slight I'd recently received turned out upon examination to be even worse than I'd originally perceived, and every subsequent mile was that much more an example of the pointless, endless obligations I'd let my life become.

Fortunately, runs like that are a once-every-few-years phenomenon. Running is the simplest, most effective way I know to go from sour to sunny in a short time. It's not the promise of a better mood that gets me out the door on difficult days; it's the near-guarantee that I'll return home in a better mood.

In previous chapters we looked at some of the long-term brain changes that running can cause. These are powerful, desirable consequences of being a runner. But on any given day, especially the tough ones, you're not concerned about the size of your hippocampus or recent gains in neuroplasticity. You just want to feel better. Running's effect on mood, how it can quickly and substantially alter your perception of your current existence, is what this chapter is about.

MOOD AND RUNNING

Mood is your subjective description of how you're feeling. In psychology, it's distinguished from emotion. Whereas emotion can be thought of as your acute reaction to a specific situation (anger, joy, disappointment, etc.), mood is a broader, longer-duration survey of your overall mental state.

Certainly events that spur emotions contribute to your mood; a thank-you card from a friend might immediately produce such emotions as happiness and surprise, but might also have a positive effect on your mood for the rest of the day, even when you're not specifically thinking about the card. But your mood can change even when the rest of the world stays the same. "If you go for a run, afterward you'll probably be happier, feel calmer, and like people better," says Frank Brooks, PhD, a clinical social worker in Portland, Maine. "That's you being in a better mood, because that's your experience of how you're operating in the world at that time."

That Brooks, a nonrunner, so accurately describes a typical postrun mood boost shows how well established the phenomenon is. Research overwhelmingly documents that people are in a better mood after exercising.[1] That's the case for both types of good moods psychologists talk about: "positive high activation" (such attributes as being alert, excited, elated, and happy) and "positive low activation" (such attributes as being content, serene, relaxed, and calm).

Running's knack for boosting mood is one of its great calling cards, no matter the state of your mental health. But it's an especially strong hook for those of us with depression or anxiety. "I cannot recall a study in which [the postexercise mood boost of] people with and without depression were compared directly," says Iowa State professor Panteleimon Ekkekakis. "What I can tell you is that the feel-better effect of a bout of exercise that is found in nondepressed individuals is also found in depressed individuals, and for statistical reasons you might assume that if you start lower you might have more of a range to improve."

That is, it's one thing to run for an hour and go from being in a good-enough mood to a better one. It's a fundamental shift to go from being miserable to content. Almost every runner I talked with for this book gave some form of Cecilia Bidwell's statement: "I'll finish a run and be like, 'Wow, this is how most people feel all the time.'" The shift I get most days is from my default fault-finding with reality to what the seminal psychologist William James called "the Yes function." I'm more expansive, open, and engaged; less sour, dismissive, and despondent.

Research on postexercise mood boost comes with a caveat: You probably need to be in decent shape for the boost to be genuine. Consider a 2009 study from George Mason University that looked at mood changes in a group of depressed men and women.[2] Immediately after a twenty-five-minute treadmill session that included fifteen minutes at a challenging pace while the treadmill was set at a 10 percent grade, the subjects said they were in a less depressed mood. But half an hour after the workout, they reported a more depressed mood and feeling less vigorous than was the case before the workout.

Why the difference between that finding and the experience of so many runners with depression? The subjects in the George Mason study were sedentary.

One of Ekkekakis' contributions to exercise psychology was the insight to perform mood surveys not only when people are done exercising, but while they're working out. From doing so, he learned "that most people, especially typical middle-aged people who tend to be overweight and have low cardiorespiratory fitness, feel worse while they exercise," he says. "Then once exercise stops there's a rebound effect— 'thank goodness it stopped.' For a few minutes after exercise, it may appear that they feel better than before they started, but that's just a bounce back from a feeling-worse effect that happens during exercise."

That's not usually the case with runners. We have the fitness needed to sustain activity below and just above what's known as the ventilatory threshold, which in practical terms Ekkekakis defines as "the point where you first start to notice a change in your respiration. Your respiration is no longer calm and irregular—it becomes deeper, more regular, more noticeable, and it changes your speaking patterns." In running terms, this is about the pace you could hold for an hour. If you're familiar with tempo runs—three to six miles at a "comfortably hard" effort level—you run them at around the intensity level Ekkekakis is talking about. "Time spent below and up to that intensity is associated with a feel-better effect," Ekkekakis says. Unfit people might reach their ventilatory threshold getting off the couch and walking across the room, so any sustained exercise is likely to have them in duress— and a worse mood—for pretty much the entire workout.

MY CHEMICAL ROMANCE

How is it that getting in your miles boosts your mood? Most people, even nonrunners, tend to give the same answer: "endorphins." In the 1970s, it became known that these chemicals, which bind to neuron receptors in the brain, are released at higher levels during a run. Several studies found that higher levels of postrun endorphins correlated to improved mood. At the height of the first running boom, endorphins became synonymous with another coinage familiar to nonrunners, the "runner's high."

It needs to be said that the "runner's high" is an imprecise concept. Ask five people to define it and you're unlikely to achieve consensus. Is an altered state where you lose track of time? A feeling of effortlessness? A state of flow? Euphoria? Being in a better mood than would seem logical given that you're working hard? The nature of research is such that scientists need agreed-upon definitions and measurable parameters. One research team has proposed "runner's high" be defined as a change in pain sensation, anxiety level, calmness, or feelings of well-being. While these criteria can be measured, running is hardly the only undertaking that can alter them. "In general, we use 'runner's high' as a catchall to get people's attention so that they know what we're talking about, more than an operational psychological state definition," says David Raichlen, PhD, a professor of anthropology at the University of Arizona who has researched runners' moods.

After the initial popularization of endorphins, most people equated them with the runner's high (however they were defining it) and considered the matter settled. Back in the lab, however, doubts began to rise as to whether the correlation between endorphin levels and mood was meaningful. After all, endorphins are released by the pituitary gland, which is located at the base of the brain but disperses its contents outside of the brain. "If endorphins have anything to do with changing how you feel, it's probably the ones in the brain, not the ones in your peripheral circulation," Ekkekakis says.

A strong correlation between endorphin levels in the brain and improved mood wasn't demonstrated until 2008.[3] German researchers used PET scans, an imaging study often used to check for cancer, on triathletes' brains while the triathletes ran for two hours. They found high levels of endorphins in the prefrontal cortex and other parts of the brain associated with mood, and that these levels aligned with the triathletes' reports of euphoria.

By that time, endorphins were no longer considered the all-purpose explanation for why most runners are mentally refreshed after a run. They're not even the only potentially relevant brain chemical. As part of his research into human evolution, Raichlen has measured pre- and postrun endocannabinoid levels in runners, dogs, and ferrets.[4] Endocannabinoids are substances that bind to the same receptors in the brain as THC, the primary substance responsible for a marijuana high.

Raichlen has found increased levels of endocannabinoids in humans and dogs following a run, but not in ferrets. That result supports the born-to-run theory on the role of running in human evolution, because the ancestors of modern humans and dogs ran to obtain food, whereas ferrets' didn't. (A side note: Raichlen found that dogs' endocannabinoid levels decreased after they walked on a treadmill for thirty minutes. It might be the case that walking your dog around the neighborhood is necessary so that Spot can do his business, but that Spot would be happier if you took him running.) Raichlen says there are two leading theories on why running causes increased levels of endorphins and endocannabinoids.

"Beginning around 1.8 to 2 million years ago, our ancestors shifted to a lifestyle that required a high level of physical activity. The changes that occur physiologically due to exercise likely are a product of that evolutionary history," he says. "Endocannabinoids and opioids are analgesics, or pain relievers. It's very possible that during exercise these neurotransmitters are activated for pain relief to allow you to move at a higher rate of speed. This would keep you moving for longer than you would without those, and a by-product would be that it makes you feel good.

"Another possibility is that this is a way that natural selection might motivate a behavior that doesn't always seem to be the smartest thing to be doing when you're a hunter-gatherer—you expend a lot of energy running, and every calorie you expend you've got to feed at some point," Raichlen continues. "At this point it's hard to figure out which of those is best supported. There's plenty of evidence from mouse models that if you do things to these neurotransmitter systems, like block them, mice that generally engage in a lot of wheel running stop doing that. So, that's suggestive that motivation is a real strong aspect of these systems. But that's not to say that we have a firm conclusion."

Raichlen agreed when I asked whether his two explanations could have coevolved. "The way that natural selection works is that things that improve reproductive success are what stay in the gene pool. So, if a combination of analgesics and neurobiological rewards to make you feel good allow someone to be a better forager, then that's going to be selected."

Of course, to be a successful hunter-gatherer, you need to be fit—it's hard to chase down an antelope or forage for three hours if you tire getting up from the Stone Age equivalent of a sofa. Raichlen's theory that feel-good brain chemicals are released during prolonged excursion meshes perfectly with the observation made earlier that runners and other trained endurance athletes have special access to mood improvement through exercise. Those brain chemicals are thought to also include such neurotransmitters as serotonin and brain-derived neurotropic factor, the protein cited in chapter 1 as associated with exercise-induced improvements in brain function.

Mood is more than a simple reflection of your current brain chemistry. When you run, your body temperature increases. Slight increases in core temperature can reduce muscle tension, which may lead to feeling more relaxed and calm, as you might be upon exiting a sauna. Body temperature can remain elevated for an hour or more after running, contributing to the "afterglow" effect.

"We tend to focus on the brain, and that's important," says J. Carson Smith, PhD, of the University of Maryland. "But after exercise the nervous system is quieter, your muscles are more relaxed, and that feeds information into your brain that you interpret as a good feeling, a state of calmness."

And let's not forget the short-term version of self-efficacy. In chapter 2, we saw how success in regularly reaching running goals, however modest, can spur a cognitive breakthrough toward life's challenges. On a day-to-day basis, postrun satisfaction with yourself for winning the battle with inertia and doing what you know is good for you can improve your mood.

THE BEST RUNS FOR MOOD BOOSTS

What types of runs will best lift your mood? How far, how fast, when, and where should you run?

Before we look at what research and best practices have to say on the matter, the most important part of the answer is "a run that occurs." It's almost always the case that any run is better than no run. Rare is the person who goes to bed thinking, "I wish I hadn't run today." The opposite scenario is familiar to most of us, especially on mentally challenging days.

Try to avoid an all-or-nothing view of running, says Brian Vasey, a clinical psychiatrist who has long used running to manage his depression and anxiety. "I used to think if I wasn't going ten miles, it wasn't worth it," he says. "I'd have a lot of days where the thought of going that far was overwhelming, and I'd take the day off. That's not helpful."

Ultramarathon star Rob Krar has also learned to overcome that approach on tough mental-health days. "In the past, if I haven't been able to get out and get done exactly what I wanted to get done, I'd be pretty hard on myself and I'd consider myself a failure," he says. "Now I'm more willing to say, 'Okay, I'm not going to be able to do that fifteen-miler or track workout, and I might miss my mileage goal for the week, but I'm going to get my ass out the door for a four-miler, even though it's nothing compared to what I'd hoped to do."

I chuckled when Krar mentioned a four-mile run. As I mentioned, I often used to be overwhelmed by the thought of being five miles from home and only halfway into a run. Those internal images sometimes resulted in taking the day off from running, which of course only made matters worse—not only was I not getting the mood boost from a run, but I felt that much more defeated by the day because I had to put "zero miles, didn't run" in my log. I've learned to tell myself that a four-miler has much more in common with a ten-miler than it does with a zero-miler.

Most studies find significant mood boosts after thirty minutes of running; for me these days, that means going at least four miles. When I'm really struggling, I start with a flexible route that can be lengthened or shortened as feels most appropriate. I try not to make any real decisions on duration until I'm at least fifteen minutes into the run. If it turns out I don't stay out much longer than that, I try to make the take-home message-to-self that I wasn't defeated, because something is better than nothing, and tomorrow will likely be better.

At the other end of the range, you may have experienced how long runs are especially effective in boosting mood. Remember, that study linking increased brain levels of endorphins with feelings of euphoria involved a two-hour run. That was an appropriate duration for the highly trained athletes in the study. But, as with most things in running, what counts as a long run is relative. For you, it might be forty minutes or seventy minutes, or whatever is a reasonable but significantly longer run than you do most days. Regardless of the length, it's the sort of run you'll feel above-and-beyond better after. When possible, I try to schedule things so that for the hour or two after a long run I can enjoy feeling like what I assume is the norm for most people.

HOW FAST?

In his research on mood-boosting endocannabinoids, Raichlen had runners do thirty-minute workouts at four effort levels.[5] He found the greatest increase in endocannabinoid levels after runs at 70 percent of maximum heart rate (which translates to jogging pace) and 80 percent of heart rate max (running at a steady, conversational pace). Endocannabinoid levels decreased after Raichlen's runners sustained 50 percent max heart rate (walking) or ran for half an hour at 90 percent of max heart rate (close to 5K race pace for many runners). For endocannabinoids, at least, it's a happy coincidence that your standard, getting-in-the-miles pace appears to be most effective. Go out for a typical workaday run, and you'll return in a better mood.

But as Raichlen himself says, "My biggest mood boosts are after tempo runs or intervals." Remember that there's more to mood than the levels of any one brain chemical. Pushing yourself through a hard workout can provide a needed sense of setting and accomplishing a goal. It's then often possible to apply that mind-set to other areas of your life when things feel overwhelming. I find it comforting to tell myself, "No matter what else happens today, I already got in six eight-hundred-meter repeats."

A Finnish study looking at opioid levels after different workout intensities is another reminder that brain chemistry doesn't necessarily trump all other contributors to mood. Researchers measured mood and opioid levels after people cycled at a moderate intensity for sixty minutes and after the subjects did a cycling interval workout (after warming up, five all-out thirty-second sprints, with four minutes of rest or easy cycling between).[6] Opioid levels were higher after the interval workout than after the moderately paced ride. But the subjects reported being in a better mood after the moderate workout. (That these people had higher opioid levels after a harder workout, in contrast to the subjects in Raichlen's study, further shows that "opioid levels" and "mood" aren't synonymous.)

Also consider a University of Wisconsin study that measured endocannabinoid levels and mood after people worked out at 70 to 75 percent of max (similar to one of the most effective levels in Raichlen's research) and at a self-selected intensity.[7] Symptoms of depression improved more when the subjects worked out at whatever intensity they wanted than when they followed the prescribed moderate intensity.

The takeaway? When you're struggling to start or continue running, allow yourself to go as slow as you want. At the other end of the spectrum, if you feel good, go!

WHEN TO RUN

For any runner, no matter the state of their mental health, the best time to run is when it's most likely to happen. The schedule of your nonrunning life is almost always going to be the final arbiter here. That schedule will likely influence not only time of day, but how many days per week.

As I mentioned in the introduction, if you run, you're a runner. There's no set number of runs per week that grants you access to or bars you from our ranks. But as I also said in the introduction, for most people, averaging at least two runs per week is a good minimum goal. That frequency will allow you to build the baseline aerobic fitness that Ekkekakis and others note is necessary to get access to many of running's feel-better effects.

As work and family obligations grow, many people find that running in the morning means less chance of things getting in the way and compromising the day's mileage. That's especially the case if you're running with others (which usually brings an added mood boost as well as help in not hitting the snooze button).

Morning might be an especially effective time for those of us whose running is key to our day-to-day mental health.

"My first couple years of being an attorney, I ran in the evening," Cecilia Bidwell says. "I loved those runs—it'd be like I'd come home super stressed out and would go for a run and then I'd feel better. But I've learned running in the morning works better because my general level of anxiety is lower overall on a daily, weekly, monthly basis. It's kind of like I've taken my pill in the morning before things get bad."

Krar says that during especially severe depressive episodes, morning runs are more effective than later ones. "If I can do that earlier in the day, I feel better about myself and it sets the trend for the rest of the day. If I can keep the momentum for the rest of that day I have a better chance of breaking out of that cycle."

I used to do my main run on workdays in late afternoon/early evening. This practice was a holdover from my time as a high school and college runner. I would often do a short run of a few miles before work, but regardless of whether that happened I would run an hour or longer after work. Through my late thirties, that schedule worked for me in terms of quality and quantity of training as well as mental-health benefits.

Now that I'm in my fifties, I'm much more of a morning runner, for two interrelated reasons. By the end of most workdays, I'm tired in a way that wasn't the case twenty-five years ago. I'm simply not going to head out for a ten-miler at 5:45 like I used to most afternoons. These days, if I don't run in the morning, my postwork runs are more like four to six miles, or thirty to fifty minutes. For me, that's my basic good-enough-for-today outing. You probably have a similar duration or length for what counts as a workaday run. Those runs are fine a few days a week, but when I string too many of them in a row, my mood suffers. I need a few longer runs to get more substantial relief, so I've switched primarily to running in the morning to make sure those extra-effective runs happen.

WHERE TO RUN

As with time of day, the location of your runs is likely to be largely determined by real-life logistics. But when you have a choice, go for the most natural setting you can find.

A lot of research has been done in recent years on the psychological response to exercise in various environments—forests, urban parks, city streets, indoors, and so on. "It appears that green spaces have a much more beneficial impact," says Raichlen. Indeed, research out of the University of Glasgow found that people who were frequently active in forests had about half the risk of poor mental health as people who didn't regularly play in the woods.[8]

For any one run, people usually report better mood improvement (more tranquility, greater reduction in stress, anxiety, and depression) in natural settings compared to populated human-made environments. One review of research on the topic found that green-space boosts were even greater when there was a water view.[9]

Neurology researcher Jeffrey Burns, MD, does a lot of his running on the treadmill during the Kansas winter. "I don't feel like I get the same benefit from that as I do from being out and letting my mind go free and being outdoors," he says of choosing Netflix over nature. Burns' experience meshes with mine. In the last four years I've run once, for all of ten minutes, on the treadmill in my garage. Despite facing frequent winter conditions like those described at the beginning of this chapter, overall it helps my head more to get outside.

"Nature" need not be miles from civilization. A 2013 study found that subjects' brains entered a more meditative state when they moved from a typical city setting to a public green space.[10] Researchers had people do a twenty-five-minute walk through Edinburgh, Scotland, while wearing a device that monitored their brain waves. The walkers started in a shopping district that has nineteenth-century buildings and light traffic. From there they walked to a park. After a stroll there they ended by walking through a busy commercial district that has lots of traffic and noise.

The walkers' brain activity varied greatly during their tour of the three urban environments. In moving from the shopping district to the park, brain activity associated with frustration, engagement, and long-term arousal fell, while activity associated with meditation rose. That changed when the walkers left the park and moved through the busy, loud commercial district. In that latter setting, one type of brain activity—"engagement or alertness with directed attention," the researchers called it—dominated.

Another chit in nature's favor: In one study, when cyclists rode a busy urban route with moderate pollution, their levels of brain-derived neurotropic factor (the "Miracle-Gro of the brain") didn't rise, in contrast to when they rode in a non-polluted setting.[11]

Natural settings can also foster mental freshness. The trails I run on are typical for New England, with roots and rocks permeating the ground. I have to stay focused on my next four footsteps if I want to stay upright, and that makes it more or less impossible to once again examine all of life's deficiencies. During the half of the year, when the trails are covered in leaves or snow, I miss this guaranteed reprieve from rumination.

Ultramarathoner Krar lives a short jog from a trailhead in Flagstaff, Arizona. Most of us have to make more of an effort to bathe ourselves in nature. But when circumstances allow, make that effort—drive to the woods on weekends, book hotels near parks when traveling. As they say at my neighborhood bakery, treat yourself, don't cheat yourself.

WHAT TO LISTEN TO

"Do you listen to music when you run?" is a common question from nonrunners.

I don't, but that's simply a matter of preference, not some claim on my part of running purity. Music is one of my main sources of pleasure in life, as is running, yet I usually find that combining the two detracts from rather than complements my enjoyment of each.

But that's just me. As in most of running, you should experiment to find what works for you, and then not worry what that supposedly says about you as a runner.

A large body of research shows that music can help several types of athletic performance. For aerobic exercise at low to moderate intensities, music can lower your perceived effort— the same pace might feel a little easier when you listen to music than when you don't. This finding is the most pertinent to whether listening to music when you run can better boost your mood. First, if you enjoy a run more, you'll probably feel better about it afterward. Second, if listening to music makes running feel easier, you might stay out longer, which should lead to greater levels of feel-good brain chemicals.

YOU DON'T HEAR ABOUT THE SWIMMER'S HIGH

Is there something uniquely effective about running for managing mental health? Or can any form of exercise provide similar relief?

The short answer is, nobody knows for sure, and definitive research comparing the mood-boosting properties of various ways of working out is unlikely. "Such a study would have multiple arms—optimal intensity, duration, or frequency of different forms of exercise—so you go from a study costing one million dollars to three million dollars," Ekkekakis says. "The pharmaceutical companies fund their own studies, but who is going to fund the exercise studies? The amount of government funding available is simply not at that level." Indeed, according to the World Health Organization, while depression is the leading cause of disability and bad health worldwide, on average only 3 percent of government health budgets is spent on mental-health issues.[12]

In terms of comparative research, the scant amount that's been done mostly consists of mood surveys of different groups of people before and after a variety of activities. That is, the people in one group might swim, others might lift weights, and others might walk. In one of the first such studies, researchers conducted mood surveys throughout a semester for undergraduate students in four different classes: introductory psychology, "jogging and conditioning," weight training, and aerobic dance.[13] (Yes, the study was done in the 1980s.) Over the course of the semester, the runners and aerobic dancers regularly reported slightly better moods than the weight lifters, and all three active groups had better mood profiles than the sedentary psych students.

Overall, aerobic exercise seems more effective than strength training. Although people report improved mood after lifting weights, much of that could stem from self-efficacy ("good for me for pushing myself like that"). Strength training, after all, doesn't induce that sustained aerobic effort that's associated with what Ekkekakis calls "the feel-better effect." Indeed, a 2016 review of research found that people with low levels of cardiovascular fitness were at greater risk of developing depression.[14]

It is safe to say that purposeful exercise is better than incidental physical activity. A study published in 2017 recorded subjects' moods over the course of a week as they exercised and engaged in what the researchers called "nonexercise activity," such as climbing stairs.[15] Predictably, their moods improved after working out. Daily-living activities not only didn't boost mood, but decreased feelings of calmness.

These various studies are interesting but don't get at what we're really interested in: How would the same people describe their mood after doing different forms of exercise? Obviously we're dealing with a self-selected population here, but the people I talked with for this book overwhelmingly supported the singular effectiveness of running.

"I've dabbled with triathlons a little," says longtime depression sufferer Rich Harfst. "I've done yoga, I've done cycling. Nothing is the same as running." Cecilia Bidwell says that when she doesn't run, her anxiety puts her basic state at a 4 out of 10. "Running normally gets me to an 8," she says. "When I'm hurt and swim instead, I'm at 6."

Heather Johnson notes an important appeal of running over other activities. "Running allows for a greater personal connection with others," she says. "It's hard to really get to know someone while swimming, dodging cars on a bike, or doing burpees. I think part of the depressed feelings I feel when I can't run may be the missing social connection."

When I asked David Raichlen about running compared to other activities, he began by citing research. "An early paper in endocannabinoid literature made the suggestion that the analgesic trigger was the mechanical pain associated with running, and that may be why swimming doesn't seem to have as big an effect," he says. "It may be that the boost from analgesic triggers is more beneficial from some sports than others." That is, the same pounding that can lead to running injuries might also result in more of a mood boost, because it spurs your body to release its natural pain-relievers more than activities with fewer impact forces.

But then the practical runner in Raichlen took over.

"It's much easier to get yourself into a reasonable intensity [while running] compared to a lot of other sports," he continues. "It's not too difficult to get in the right zone and stay there. You have a lot more control over your speed than even in something like cycling, where your effort level is more dictated by the topography or even stop lights." Also, unlike such activities as swimming or Nordic skiing, running doesn't require learning technique well enough to sustain the right effort level.

The University of Maryland's J. Carson Smith offers an intriguing theory: "One thing that distinguishes running is the feedback that's received by pounding on your feet. Studies in mice show that there are direct neural pathways that respond to the foot hitting the ground. They send information that is eventually communicated to the sympathetic nervous systems of the brain, and that feedback has an influence on how those brain regions are storing, synthesizing, and releasing neurotransmitters like serotonin."

Krar, who cycles and competes in ski mountaineering, agrees about the primacy of running: "Ski mountaineering is much more an anaerobic effort [than running]. It's much harder to find that flow state and go on and on at a comfortable, meditative pace. Mountain biking is loud, it's mechanical, it's not as free and natural. Running is that perfect balance where you can push yourself as hard as you like, and it's easier to get into that flow state, problem-solve, be one with nature, and hear your breathing and footsteps."

My longest experiment with other activities came in the first half of 2013, before and after foot surgery. Mostly I cycled, ten to twelve hours a week on a trainer in the basement. I rode outside as well, but indoors gave me much greater control over my effort level, for the reasons Raichlen cites. I thought of each pedal stroke as a stitch in a safety net that would keep my day-to-day mood from sinking too low.

But there was little in the way of the acute spikes I feel during or after running. Staring at the basement wall an hour or two a day was simply something that needed to be done to stay sane and fit. I wound up not running for five months; since I started in 1979, the longest I'd previously gone without a run was two weeks. When, in September 2013, I ran for an hour for the first time in nine months, I cried afterward. I knew I again had access to the most reliable, convenient, and immediate source of relief from my depression.

CHAPTER 5

Running and Antidepressants

In the late spring of 1994, Alberto Salazar made running headlines for the first time in years. A dozen years before, he'd been one of the world's top distance runners, with three straight wins at the New York City Marathon (one in a then world best) and the celebrated "Duel in the Sun" victory by two seconds at the 1982 Boston Marathon. Never the prettiest runner to watch, Salazar succeeded in part by sheer force of will, epitomized by pushing himself so hard one year at the Falmouth Road Race that he was administered last rites.

Salazar's body eventually began to betray him. In 1983, he placed fifth in a couple of international marathons—still excellent performances, but not the dominance fans had come to expect—and he placed last in the ten-thousand-meter final of the world championships. In 1984, he was outkicked for the win at the US Olympic Marathon Trials by a then unknown Pete Pfitzinger, whose personal best was more than three minutes slower than Salazar's. In the Olympic Marathon, Salazar was never a factor. Running with uncharacteristic caution, he placed fifteenth, beaten again by Pfitzinger. Salazar gave up marathoning, got slower and slower in shorter races, and eventually stopped competing.

Imagine the surprise, then, in late May 1994 when word began to trickle out that Salazar had won the Comrades Marathon in South Africa, a fifty-six-mile race that's arguably the most prestigious ultramarathon in the world. Imagine further the surprise when, in postrace interviews, Salazar ascribed some of his resurgence to the antidepressant medication Prozac.

"It had an almost immediate effect on my general overall health," Salazar told me in 1994 for an article in the now-defunct magazine *Running Times*. "My ability to handle stress was back to where it used to be, and my energy levels went way up." He said he began taking Prozac on the recommendation of two doctors to restore his energy levels. "I never felt depressed," Salazar said about his pre-Prozac condition, "but I felt like life was harder than it should be. I always saw myself as a type A person who thrived on doing a lot, but now I was just tired all the time." He told me he started feeling better—and running better—just three days after going on Prozac.

Salazar's story struck me in two ways. First, in researching to write about the topic, I read a lot about symptoms of depression. In the pre-Google age, finding DIY diagnostics wasn't as easy as it is now. I looked over lists of symptoms, which included such things as hopelessness, lethargy, and lack of interest in ordinary activities, and paused. Didn't everyone feel this way most of the time? My default state isn't the norm? The process led to more reading and set into motion the realization of my own longtime condition that I've detailed elsewhere in this book.

My second takeaway from Salazar's story: I can take a pill and feel better? And my running will improve? Sign me up!

In the two-plus decades since, the intersection of antidepressants and running has become both much more common and much more nuanced. In this chapter, we'll look at what modern antidepressants aim to do and what's known, via research and anecdotal reports, about how they affect running.

ANTIDEPRESSANTS ARE EVERYWHERE

Salazar was an early adopter of the modern class of antidepressants known as selective serotonin reuptake inhibitors, often called SSRIs. (Some well-known modern antidepressants aren't SSRIs; we'll get to that in the next section.) These antidepressants are now typically prescribed before older classes, such as tricyclics, are tried, because the older drugs usually have greater side effects.

These days, the drugs are far from obscure. According to the most recent data from the Centers for Disease Control and

Prevention (CDC), antidepressants are among the three most commonly prescribed classes of drugs in the United States.[1] (The other two are pain relievers and medications for high cholesterol.) Between 2011 and 2014, 12.7 percent of Americans aged twelve or older reported taking an antidepressant in the previous month. That was a significant increase from 1999, when the equivalent figure was 7.7 percent.

Antidepressant use varies greatly by age and gender. In the CDC data, women are almost twice as likely as men to report using an antidepressant in the previous month (16.5 percent to 8.6 percent). Usage climbs with age: 3.4 percent in people ages 12 to 19, 7.8 percent for ages 20 to 39, 16.6 percent for ages 40 to 59, and 19.1 percent for ages 60 and over.

There are also differences by ethnic origin. In the CDC data, non-Hispanic whites are five times more likely than non-Hispanic Asians to have taken antidepressants in the past month (16.5 percent and 3.3 percent, respectively) and three times more likely than Hispanics (5.0 percent) and non-Hispanic blacks (5.6 percent). The highest usage appears to be among non-Hispanic white women (21.4 percent) and women aged sixty and over (24.4 percent).

Current usage trends indicate Americans view antidepressants as a long-term medication. The CDC finds that, of people who take an antidepressant, 44 percent report doing so for at least the last five years. A quarter of antidepressant users say they've been on medication for ten or more years.

The CDC numbers don't break down usage by income. That information would likely support the contention of

Panteleimon Ekkekakis, a professor at Iowa State University, that antidepressants are both over- and underprescribed in the United States.

"The majority of antidepressants in the United States are given to people for non-depression-related diagnoses," he says. "They're prescribed for all kinds of things—fatigue, fibromyalgia, eating disorders, obsessive-compulsive disorder, anxiety." A 2009 study found that almost 80 percent of antidepressant prescriptions are written by physicians others than psychiatrists.

"The pharmaceutical companies have created this impression that antidepressants might help but they generally don't hurt anybody," Ekkekakis says. "So, some physicians will say, 'I'll give you something else for whatever you have, but I'm also going to give you an antidepressant just in case.' In the US, only about 25 percent of prescriptions are based on depression-specific complaints or a depression diagnosis. In that sense, they're overprescribed.

"But there's not the same approach with people who don't have good insurance coverage," Ekkekakis continues. "In the lower socioeconomic strata, where depression is likely to be more prevalent, antidepressants are underprescribed."

HOW ANTIDEPRESSANTS WORK

The popularity of modern antidepressants is especially striking when you consider that experts aren't sure exactly why they work.

Although SSRIs are commonly used to represent all modern antidepressants, there are newer types that affect the reuptake of other neurotransmitters besides serotonin. SNRIs work on both serotonin and norepinephrine; examples include Effexor and Cymbalta. Bupropion, which is the generic name for Wellbutrin, is a norepinephrine-dopamine reuptake inhibitors (NDRI). (In this chapter I'll mostly use brand names of antidepressants.)

What these drugs have in common is that they're designed to change the behavior of neurotransmitters, which are chemicals that help brain cells communicate. Specifically, antidepressants keep neurotransmitters thought to be associated with mood regulation from getting immediately reabsorbed into the brain's nerve cells after they've done their transmission work (hence "reuptake inhibitor"). For example, the drugs may keep serotonin in the space between nerve cells, or synapses, for longer. The increased presence of neurotransmitters in synapses is thought to spur other activity in the brain that leads to a reduction in the symptoms of depression.

"The surprising part is that people are not quite sure how these changes in neurotransmission link to depression," Ekkekakis says. As we saw in chapter 2, it appears that depression is linked with shrinkage in the area of the brain called the hippocampus, which is primarily involved with memory. In people who take antidepressants, the hippocampus tends to show neuroplasticity, or the creation of new neurons, and an increase in the size of the hippocampus.

"The degree of the neuroplasticity and the degree of the size of the restoration of the hippocampus appears to be related to the antidepressant effect," explains Ekkekakis. "The reason I say it's complicated is because we don't understand why an area of the brain that appears to be involved with memory would somehow contribute to an antidepressant effect."

If those brain changes sound familiar, that's because they're the same ones often found in depressed people who start exercising. Antidepressants, in other words, appear to improve the same part of the brain that running is thought to.

There's also debate about how well antidepressants work, and for whom. Studies on the drugs' effectiveness usually focus on reduction of symptoms (e.g., feeling sad less often) rather than broader outcomes (e.g., functioning well in everyday life). Whether that difference bothers you probably depends in part on what you expect from antidepressants—to make life more bearable versus to make you depression-free. I lean strongly toward the former, partly because I wouldn't expect a drug to "cure" me any more than I expect running to. Also, for me there's not a clear difference between the two goals. If I'm sad less often, I tend to function better in everyday life.

The biggest criticism about antidepressants' effectiveness is that, especially in cases of mild depression, they're either only slightly more or no more effective than placebos.[2] That is, people on an antidepressant may report no more reductions in symptoms than might people taking a placebo.

Given the side effects that can accompany antidepressants, such as sexual dysfunction and weight changes, some experts have concluded that the risks outweigh the benefits.

It's important to remember that a placebo effect is still an effect. When I told clinical psychiatrist and runner Brian Vasey about Salazar's quick reaction to Prozac, he said, "I wouldn't dispute that he felt better in three days. The placebo effect is pretty powerful."

This line of thinking should be familiar to runners. Say you committed to getting half an hour more sleep on weeknights in your buildup to your last half marathon, and that you ran faster in that half than in your previous one despite your training being similar. Did the extra sleep help? Better stated, did sleeping more allow you to better absorb and recover from your training, and therefore improve your fitness come race day?

Or was it the idea of the extra sleep—"Look how dedicated I am to this race, going to bed earlier to prepare for it"—that really made the difference? In the latter scenario, the regular reminder that you were trying to get better could create a positive feedback loop: You tell yourself you're recovering better, so you push a little harder in your workouts, and progress there motivates you to eat a little better, and losing a couple pounds makes your long runs feel better, and nailing your long runs gets you excited about race day, and so on.

The same sort of self-reinforcing cycle is possible with antidepressants. Telling yourself that you're finally doing something about your condition—in this case, taking medication—can be the catalyst for improving that condition. In this vein, it's interesting to note that, in trials of antidepressants, placebo effects have greatly increased over time. That increase coincides with growing societal acceptance of the drugs. If you know more people who say they feel better after starting on antidepressants, and if there's less stigma with antidepressants than there used to be, it's possible that a placebo effect is more likely.

HOW DO ANTIDEPRESSANTS AFFECT RUNNING?
Salazar's story from the mid-1990s made the potential performance-enhancing benefits of antidepressants a common topic in running for a while. While cautioning about such benefits for all the reasons we're about to see, Ekkekakis says, "Theoretically speaking, it would make some sense. There are a lot of indications that serotonin is involved in fatigue, and therefore if you optimize serotonin neurotransmission, it could theoretically change the sense of tiredness."

But as Ekkekakis told me while we discussed health research in general, how taking antidepressants for their prescribed reasons affects the training and racing of everyday runners isn't the sort of topic that gets priority funding. The pharmaceutical companies that make the medications focus their research on such things as the drugs' effectiveness in treating various conditions, relatively benign common side effects, and uncommon but potentially dangerous side effects. Other health researchers need to convince grant providers that their area of inquiry meets an important public-health need. Whether Wellbutrin makes a fifty-three-year-old recreational runner like me a little faster or slower in his next race isn't considered vital.

The executive summary is that what research there has been is equivocal. There's no mountain of evidence showing that antidepressants significantly improve or decrease exercise performance. Why the uncertainty?

"One thing about serotonin is you can find people who say the higher the serotonin, the higher the sense of fatigue, and you can find people who say the higher the level, the lower the sense of fatigue," Ekkekakis says. "So, exactly how the serotonin levels and [what area of] the brain are related to fatigue is unclear. What appears to be clear is that there's some involvement, but that's about the extent of it."

Further adding to the lack of clarity:

* Many of the studies have used a small number of subjects, which can make extrapolating from them to the population as a whole unreliable.

* Most of the subjects in studies were men; their results wouldn't necessarily be duplicated by women.

* Some studies have used as subjects athletes who wouldn't merit an antidepressant prescription in real life.

* Some studies look at elements of exercise performance after a single dosage, which is, of course, not necessarily the same as being on an antidepressant for the rest of your life.

* Some studies use the maximum safe dosage of an antidepressant, so any effect could be different than at the lower

dosage most people take. (The motivation behind some of these studies is to see whether antidepressants impart enough of a performance benefit to merit falling under antidoping regulations in elite sport.)

* As is often the case in the lab, many studies use cycling rather than running as the form of exercise.

* Some of the studies have all of these elements—they look at the performance of a small number of male cyclists who don't need an antidepressant after a single, safe-maximum dosage.

Another caveat is that, by necessity, studies use one antidepressant. Even an unambiguous finding about, say, Paxil's effect on core body temperature during hard exercise isn't necessarily transferable to Prozac or Wellbutrin or Lexapro.

And before we look at specific studies, it's important to remember just how complex a system your body on the run is. A change in one measurable parameter, such as core body temperature, may or may not result in better or worse performance. Conversely, sometimes lab studies find differences in performance between two conditions even when variables such as blood glucose levels and carbohydrate metabolism are the same. This ambiguity can be frustrating if you're looking for clear, black-and-white answers. But it's heartening for those of us who consider running performance more than the predictable outcome of a series of quantifiable inputs.

Studies on endurance performance tend to use either time trials (how fast you can complete a given distance) or time-to-exhaustion trials (how long you can sustain a given exercise intensity). Time trials are generally more applicable to the real world; they're a solo simulation of racing, while few of us encounter situations where we run at a set pace for as long as possible and then stop when we have to slow.

When the studies have been conducted in normal environmental conditions, Prozac, Paxil, Celexa, and Wellbutrin have not improved time-trial or time-to-exhaustion performance. In one study, the more aerobically fit subjects performed significantly worse on a time-to-exhaustion cycling trial after taking a single 20-milligram dose of Paxil.[3]

There has been research indicating that a single large dose (300 milligrams, considered the maximum safe amount) of Zyban improves performance in very hot conditions. (Zyban is a brand name for bupropion, which is what's also in Wellbutrin.) In one study done in conditions of 86 degrees Fahrenheit and 48 percent humidity, men rode almost 5 percent faster in a cycling time trial when they took that maximal dosage of Zyban instead of a placebo.[4] A similar study with women duplicated the findings. The performance benefit didn't follow more normal doses (150 or 225 milligrams). Of note is that after all the Zyban time trials, the subjects' core temperature was higher. At the end of the maximum-dose trial, their heart rate was higher, which makes sense given that they wound up riding faster. The researchers wrote, "Despite an increase in core temperature and improved performance in the maximal dose, there was no change in [perceived effort] and thermal sensation, suggesting an altered motivation or drive to continue."

Again, though, this was a single, safe-maximum dose, given to people who didn't necessarily merit a prescription. That's more the stuff of doping than real-world relevance. When the same researchers repeated the study after subjects took Zyban for ten days, the performance benefit wasn't duplicated, and the subjects' core temperature wasn't as high as during the single-dosage study.[5] "It seems that chronic administration results in an adaptation of central neurotransmitter homeostasis, resulting in a different response to the drug," the researchers wrote.

Probably the more important finding stemming from that research is the increase in core temperature after taking Zyban. A study involving Paxil in warm conditions also found an increase in core temperature.[6] In the Zyban study, the finding that the athletes' "thermal sensation" didn't change means that they didn't feel hotter despite a higher core temperature. Such a mismatch could lead to the improved performance seen in the acute study, but it could also lead to problems if you're doing a long run on an 85-degree day and don't feel warm even though your core temperature is approaching a dangerous level. Heat intolerance is among the potential side effects listed for some antidepressants, including Wellbutrin and other brands of bupropion. We'll return to this matter later in this chapter.

So far, we've looked at research on how antidepressants might affect your running. This field of inquiry—how drugs affect the body—is known as pharmacodynamics. But what about flipping the equation? Are there ways in which being a runner can affect the antidepressant you might be taking? Might runners need different dosages than sedentary people?

After all, prescriptions often take into account physical traits of the patient, such as age, weight, ethnicity, and pregnancy status. Given that exercise is often recommended in conjunction with other treatments for depression and anxiety, and given that many of us are self-medicating with running, the issue of whether regular running might alter an antidepressant's efficacy is hardly esoteric. Unfortunately, the relevant research on what's known as pharmacokinetics—how bodies affect drugs—is even more scant concerning antidepressants and athletes.

One of the few people to investigate the issue is Ethan Ruderman. For his master's thesis in kinesiology at the University of Toronto, Ruderman examined whether exercise appeared to affect bodily processing of a single dose of sertraline (most commonly known by the brand name Zoloft).[7]

Ruderman had fourteen men in their twenties take 100 milligrams of sertraline on two occasions, at least two weeks apart: once while resting and once before cycling for thirty minutes at a moderate intensity. Ruderman collected blood samples over the ensuing forty-eight hours. When the men exercised after taking the medication, the elimination half-life of the drug changed; that is, it remained in their body longer.

Part of the explanation for this finding could be differences in blood flow when we're resting versus working out. When you run, blood is diverted from some body parts to working muscles (to supply them with more oxygen) and the skin (to help with cooling). That phenomenon is why it can be unpleasant to run too soon after eating—the usual blood flow to your stomach is reduced, so food just sits there instead of being digested. When you run, there's also a lot less blood going to your liver, which plays a key role in metabolizing medications. It's possible, then, running could slow the rate at which you metabolize antidepressants (or other medications, for that matter). It's also possible that long-term changes brought on by being a runner, such as greater density of the tiny blood vessels known as capillaries and lower body fat concentration, could affect how a drug makes its way through your body.

Ruderman is careful not to make definitive statements about the implications of his study. Instead, he hopes his work will spur more research on and awareness of how exercise might affect medications' effectiveness. "[B]oth the acute bouts of exercise and the fact that people might be a marathoner with a very different fitness status should be included in the conversation—along with height, weight, age, ethnicity—when you're talking about dosage," he says.

In my work as a running journalist and book author, I often read research on exercise performance. A big takeaway from decades of doing that is that exercise science is sometimes most helpful in explaining what runners already do, as opposed to discovering what runners should do. For example, runners were doing tempo runs—three to six miles at a "comfortably hard" pace, somewhere between fifteen-kilometer and marathon race pace—long before exercise scientists delineated that these runs can improve your ability to clear lactate, an adaptation that helps you hold a strong pace for longer.

That's how I think about the current state of research on running and antidepressants. We runners will figure it out in the ultimate lab of daily road work. Ideally, researchers will one day explain the why. But for now, the best we have to go on are one another's experiences. So, here is mine and those of several fellow runners.

MY EXPERIENCE AS A RUNNER ON ANTIDEPRESSANTS

I first saw a psychiatrist in early 1995. (I later learned he wasn't accepting new patients, but as a runner he was intrigued about working with the editor of *Running Times*, the magazine I was then the editor of.) Before the end of our initial session, he said I was a good candidate for an antidepressant.

I was initially prescribed Zoloft. Like Salazar, I felt almost immediate effects, but of the opposite sort—a near-catatonic haze that made me feel like I was pawing through a stream of molasses. For several days I canceled all work and social plans and spent almost all my time in bed. (Almost: I got out for a dutiful three-mile jog each day.) The severity of the haze eventually lessened, but never disappeared, and after a month I started cycling off Zoloft.

Next, I tried Prozac. Within a month, three longtime features of my dysthymia abated. First, I slept better. Pre-Prozac,

I woke several times a night, usually with one or more of those occurrences lasting for a while. While awake, I could cram a day's worth of rumination into half an hour: What is the point of going about my business tomorrow? Why is everything so hard? Why can't I enjoy life the way others seem to? Is this how it's going to be the next fifty years? Once I was on Prozac, those incidents continued, but weren't as frequent, because I wasn't awake every hour.

Second, Prozac seemed to do its trademark thing of eliminating the lowest lows. My thousand-yard-stare days, when it felt as if a backhoe loader had scraped out the happier parts of my brain and left a pit, almost entirely went away.

Finally, for the preceding several years, I'd often felt like one of those figurine toys held together by string that collapse when you push on the bottom. Being on Prozac, I told my psychiatrist, made me feel tauter, more efficient in navigating the world, that nobody was pressing on the bottom of the string toy. ("Interesting," he replied. "You're the second person this week to mention those toys.")

Side effects seemed minimal: I lost a pound or two (unnecessary but not detrimental for a 130-pounder) and my libido dropped (overall, a welcome change for a single thirty-one-year-old man without a girlfriend).

I waited for a Salazaresque running resurgence, but it never came, even with markedly better sleep. In fact, the only discernible effect on my running was negative. Once on Prozac, I stopped digging down that last 1 or 2 percent in the final third of races. After the first few times it happened,

I wondered whether the phenomenon was physiological or psychological. With more time on the medication, I decided it was the latter. As I said, Prozac lopped off my lowest lows, which was much appreciated. The price for that was paid from the other end of the spectrum; I also lost my highest highs. Prozac made me more nonchalant, less intense about pretty much everything, including, I realized, whether I ran that weekend's 5K seven seconds faster.

Several years later, Olympian Adam Goucher reported the same running reaction to an antidepressant. Goucher eventually said that, as a professional athlete, he couldn't justify that effect, and went off the medication. In my early thirties and very focused on my work when I went on Prozac, I knew I was a few years past setting my last personal record. I decided any trade-off of racing a little slower for overall life improvement was worth it for me. I might have decided differently if I'd thought I still had some PRs in me. (A side note: I never regained that lost edge, even during times I wasn't on antidepressants.)

One thing that did happen as soon as I started taking antidepressants: I decided to be open about it. My analogy at the time was that my father had an inherited cholesterol problem that merited medication, and I had an inherited mental-health issue that merited medication. Why should I be any more coy or secretive about the treatment of my condition than my father was about his?

Soon after, I wrote a short essay about my dysthymia and medication for *Running Times*. The reaction mainly took two forms. I heard from people thanking me for my candor, and heard from others saying I was a head case who was looking for an easy way to avoid life's problems. Both types of responses bolstered my decision to be open and potentially play a small part in reducing the stigma of mental-health issues and their many forms of treatment.

For the next decade and a half, I cycled on and off Prozac. Despite my cholesterol medication analogy, there was always part of me that didn't like the idea of taking a pill every day for the rest of my life. Every few years I'd feel ready to try life without Prozac. Varying amounts of time would pass until I'd realize the balance between good-enough days and too-miserable days was once again out of whack, independent of the state of my running, my marriage, and other aspects of life. When I slumped into their office, no doctor ever needed convincing to write me a prescription.

But each time, Prozac seemed less effective. In the spring of 2011 I started on it again; that turned out to be the last time.

As I've mentioned, my dysthymia has never majorly interfered with my professional productivity. But this time, Prozac did. I'd sit in front of my laptop and watch myself not care that I didn't care I was goofing off instead of working. Deadlines came and went, emails went unanswered, collaborative projects arrived at my desk to die. And all I felt capable of doing was thinking, "Well, isn't this interesting?" To be clear, I don't really like working, but I'd always been dependable. Now I felt like a stoner. It was the first time a medication made me feel like someone other than myself.

I cycled off Prozac, started taking Wellbutrin, and still do. It's had no noticeable effect on my running, good or bad. I've always been a ridiculously heavy sweater, so if Wellbutrin has made my heat tolerance worse, I'm unaware of it. (I might feel differently if I lived in Texas, not Maine.)

More important, the medication seems to help with daily life with minimal side effects—resting heart rate increase of a few beats, occasional light sensitivity—so I'd probably stay on it even if I felt it made me a worse hot-weather runner. That trade-off would be acceptable nearly four decades into my running career. For the foreseeable future, I'm over my trepidation about permanently being on an antidepressant.

OTHER RUNNERS' EXPERIENCES WITH ANTIDEPRESSANTS

There's great variance in how other runners feel on and about antidepressants.

For Ryan Rathbun, an engineer from Chicago, antidepressants improved his running in the most direct way possible—by helping him get off the couch and out the door.

Rathbun ran track in middle school and high school, then mostly switched to other sports, including rugby, in college. "When I got out in the working world all that exercise stuff kind of faded away," he says. "There were at least ten years where I did nothing. I grew fatter and more depressed, started drinking too much, and just slowly went downhill. I had relationship problems and an existential crisis, and hit rock bottom." His then partner told Rathbun, "You need to change," and he agreed.

Rathbun had been on antidepressants (Prozac and Wellbutrin) before, with mixed results. Working with a therapist, he started on Cymbalta, and once he got the dosage right, felt a profound difference. "All the other times were, 'Yeah, I'm better, but eh . . . ,'" he says. "This one was, 'Oh, this is how normal people feel? This is a lot different.'"

After some time on the medication, Rathbun was drinking less and eating better (including no longer binge eating). He thought, "Hey, I've lost a ton of weight here. I could start exercising again." He picked a goal race and revived his running career. He's now a competitive age-group racer, especially in skyscraper stairwell climbs. "It doesn't feel like I'm relying on this," he says about his current medication. "I feel like the person I always thought I was or should be."

Like Rathbun, Rebecca Skoczylas, a school psychologist from a Detroit suburb, started regular running only after going on antidepressants. But she says her running doesn't necessarily stem from her medications (Lexapro and Wellbutrin).

"I began taking meds three weeks after my second child was born and began running just a few months later," she says of taking up the sport in 2007. "I can tell you that there is no way that the meds sufficiently address all my symptoms. When I have had a really rough day, there is nothing that can help me like a good, hard run. And there is no way that the immediate high and satisfaction I get from a long run is only from the meds." The biggest effect of medication on her running the seven-time marathoner notices is that she has, she says, "an easier time staying motivated when the med situation is under control."

Skoczylas had surgery in 2016 to remove a large, cancerous tumor. She increased her dosage because of increased anxiety. But, she says, running, not medication, really brought her around: "I did not feel 'normal' again until I was back to running."

Jeff Lee, an accountant from Hartselle, Alabama, says that his medication helps his running, but he discovered that's the case in a roundabout way.

Lee has been on Effexor (and occasionally Klonopin) for more than ten years for chronic depression and anxiety. He began running a few years ago at age forty-nine to lose weight and improve his health. Late in 2016, he decided to stop taking the medications. "I had been on it a long time, was healthier, and was running thirty to thirty-five miles per week, so I hoped I didn't need it anymore," he says.

Within a couple of weeks, Lee reports, his mental state was what it had been a decade ago: "I can't tell I'm on it until I'm off it."

He resumed taking the medications, and during the several weeks it took for them to take effect, "it was everything I could do to make myself run, but I did," Lee says. He realized "I run more and have more interest [in running] while using my medicine."

The intersection of Ali Nolan's running and medication is more complex. A former *Runner's World* colleague of mine, the Dallas resident went on Lexapro in 2016 to address increasingly intrusive anxiety. The medication vastly improved her nonrunning life. "I no longer have reoccurring thoughts of doom or the feeling of being trapped," Nolan says. "Most days I can get to sleep. I also can do my work without having to take forty breaks to make dozens of checklists. I can read again—kind of important for a writer/editor."

Things were more complicated with her running. Nolan says she has been able to enjoy her running more after going on medication, and that overall this was a welcome development: "For a very, very long time, running was the only thing that I used to manage my symptoms. That lasted until I realized I was running too much and running a lot of garbage miles and that running itself was becoming a sort of compulsion and source of anxiety."

But greater balance came with some costs in performance, especially at the end of races. "I think that I am moving slower than I used to," she says. Also, "I eat a lot more cake now. Seriously, the sweet cravings are terrible. I estimate I've gained five pounds."

In general, "the problem is that I'm so relaxed about it," Nolan says. "If I miss a run, I shrug it off. I used to get really upset about missing miles and would fret about it for days. To avoid that feeling, I wouldn't skip a day. Now I'm so casual about it. I think that that might be because the run isn't carrying such weight in my mental wellness anymore. It's purely for enjoyment and fitness. Before, if I missed a run, I would feel like the world was ending, plus I'd feel like a failure because I missed the run. Now I guess I'm more like a 'normal' person."

Nolan says she's willing to accept the trade-offs for now, given that overall her life has improved. But, she says, "If I ever felt too sluggish or too apathetic to run, that would be an issue. I suppose if I dipped under twelve miles per week and didn't care, I'd have my husband check my pulse to make sure I was still alive."

We'll end this admittedly unscientific survey with Amelia Gapin, who has an interesting take on how antidepressants improve her running. She has always valued how her usual depressive and anxious ruminations eventually disappear when she runs. Now that welcome process starts sooner.

"It doesn't seem to take as long into a run for the depression and anxiety to lift away," Gapin says. Since starting on medication, "a lot of the low-level, background daily stuff is diminished, so when I go for a run I'm starting in a much better place—mentally I might be starting, where before I'd be at like two miles into a run."

OPTING OUT
In interviewing runners for this book, I heard from several who have eschewed antidepressants.

Some, like Cecilia Bidwell of Tampa, Florida, don't like the idea of taking psychotropic drugs and find that their running and other practices sufficiently manage their condition. Bidwell, who has anxiety, says, "I don't mean this in any way as judgment of people who go that route, but I do think that things like SSRIs alter brain chemistry. For some people, that's necessary to get through the day. But if I can get enough sleep, if I can keep my job under control, if I can get out and run every day, I can handle all that and life is good and I shouldn't have to resort to something else. This is the real me, and I'm afraid [medication] would change my personality and make me someone I'm not."

My running partner Kristin Barry has a similar take. When her lifelong depression became especially strong in her first year of law school, Barry tried medication, but stopped after two weeks. "They made me feel like I had too much caffeine—jittery, on edge, shaky," she says. "I was hesitant to take medication anyway, so it was easy to stop when I felt like I was having a bad reaction."

In the two decades since, Barry has relied on her running (she's a 2:40 marathoner who twice qualified for the Olympic Marathon Trials) and therapy to manage her depression. When she was setting personal bests earlier this decade, some of her reluctance came from concern about how medication might affect her running. (I'd told her many times about how antidepressants seemed to rob me of the desire to go to the well late in races.)

These days, she says, "my reluctance stems from a general avoidance, if possible, of all medications. I do not like the idea of messing with my brain chemistry, even though what I am working with is not an ideal brain chemistry to have. I realize that's not a great mentality. It's kind of like ignoring a wound. I try to manage it as best as I can without meds, but if I were to have another episode like 1997, I would not be against taking them, especially now, as a parent."

Brian Frain, a mutual fund analyst from Milwaukee, is uneasy about the bodily effects of medication, and not just antidepressants. "I'm concerned about altering my body's chemistry," he says. "I've always been averse to any medication. I don't even take aspirin! I understand that medications are designed to help, but I'm always concerned about how things will interact, long-term. Antidepressants in general can be extremely powerful and the long-term side effects can't be known at this time. I worry about them throwing my entire system off balance, which will undoubtedly hurt my running in the end."

Another of my running partners, Heather Johnson, also tries to avoid medications of any type, despite a lifetime of sometimes severe anxiety. "One of the biggest reasons I haven't really gone down the med route is that I have a fear of side effects. I don't really take anything, including herbal remedies," she says. When I asked her what would constitute unacceptable interference from medication in her running, she said, "Within reason, I'd say anything is unacceptable interference. [Running] is my sanity. I have to put it first and realize that it helps me cope with so much. I'm a better mom, wife, and friend if I run."

A TRUE EXPERIMENT OF ONE

All of the above—antidepressants' effectiveness versus their side effects, how medication might affect your running, and runners' varying experiences with antidepressants—underlies the lack of black-and-white rules on how to proceed here. Common side effects of antidepressants, such as weight gain or loss, dry mouth, and drowsiness, as well as rarer ones, such as heat intolerance, could be more significant for you as a runner than for a sedentary person. And unlike a sedentary person, you'll need to consider the balancing act between help from a medication and how it might hurt the self-medication known as your running.

If you're lucky, you'll find a doctor knowledgeable enough and willing to account for your running when considering a prescription. A 2016 survey of members of the International Society for Sports Psychiatry found that such doctors exist.[8] On the whole, these physicians said they "tended to favor medications that are relatively more energizing and less likely to cause sedation, weight gain, cardiac side effects, and tremor." (The doctors were surveyed about medications for a variety of mental-health conditions rather than just depression and anxiety.)

"[P]rescribing preferences for athletes diverged from many of the prescribing trends seen for patients within the general population, in keeping with the assumption that different factors are considered when prescribing for athletes versus for the general population," the authors of the survey concluded.

Brian Vasey says that, for all of his patients, he first explores whether they've responded to alternative treatments. If he decides medication is warranted, he tries to address the most significant symptoms with minimal side effects. For runners, Vasey says, "SSRIs like sertraline [brand name Zoloft], fluoxetine [Prozac], and citalopram [Celexa] can potentially negatively affect motivation. I would have a conversation with the athlete about the risks of taking one of these in that he or she might feel less driven but might feel less sad, depressed, or anxious."

Vasey counsels patience in the early days of taking antidepressants: "Give the medicine a little bit of time to see how it goes, because often side effects lessen over time. I see side effects lessening for some after ten to fourteen days, just about the time when positive and hoped-for medical effects are beginning to be seen. Generally, though, for full benefits we need to wait four to six weeks. If side effects are intolerable I would not be hesitant to stop and switch medicines."

If you do decide to try antidepressants, it's worth remembering that they're usually most effective as part of a multitier approach. As a runner, you already have a key form of symptom management. But there are others worth exploring as well. In the next several chapters, we'll look at the intersection of running and several nonpharmaceutical forms of treatment for depression and anxiety.

CHAPTER 6

Running and Talk Therapy

A friend of mine's third date with her now-husband was a run—a great way to turbocharge getting to know someone. Despite the popular perception of runners as taciturn loners, we love sharing the miles. (Well, most of us do—my friend's husband told her after their date that he prefers to run solo.) Key to that appeal are the conversations we have when running with others.

One of the most interesting things about those conversations is how naturally they come about. Even when meeting someone for the first time, I don't have the what-will-we-talk-about worries before a run that I do before sedentary social outings. Another interesting thing about talking on the run is that you frequently find yourself discussing the most personal issues—relationships, work, family, and, for good measure, the meaning of life. Doing so can feel safer and the words often come out better when you're running than at other times.

Those of us who have had these intimate mobile conversations as well as professional talk therapy have noticed their similarities. In this chapter we'll look at how runners with depression and anxiety can best benefit from both.

WHAT IS TALK THERAPY?

Talk therapy is the most common type of psychotherapy, a form of treatment provided by psychologists, psychiatrists, and licensed counselors for a broad range of mental-health and other issues. When someone says they're seeing a therapist, they usually mean that they're having talk therapy sessions.

Modern talk therapy is not lying on a couch recounting your dreams while an inscrutable Austrian man reminds you that sometimes a cigar is just a cigar. Talk therapy entails goal-oriented collaborative work between patient and professional to improve specific aspects of the patient's life. Therapists help patients articulate issues that are lowering their quality of life. Once key problems are defined, therapists help patients learn to think about and address those problems in research-backed ways. A common goal of talk therapy is for patients to replace old habits of thinking and doing with healthier habits.

Talk therapy is well established as a frontline treatment for depression[1] and anxiety.[2] Many experts believe it to be more effective than medication, especially in mild to moderate cases. You might recall news stories from a few years ago that the effectiveness of talk therapy has been overstated. What was missing from many of the headlines was that the study the reports were based on concluded that talk therapy is efficacious "but not to the extent that the published literature would suggest."[3] According to this review of research, talk therapy gives people a 20 percent greater chance of improvement, not a 30 percent chance, as previously thought. I'll take those odds.

One key to benefiting from talk therapy is, well, talking. Little progress is possible if you and the therapist don't have access to your core triggers for and manifestations of depression or anxiety. Runners with depression or anxiety might have a head start in talk therapy because we have so much experience examining life's issues in an intense but set-duration environment. When I first saw a therapist for depression in 1995, I was immediately comfortable with being completely open. I already had more than fifteen years of droning on to a captive audience, and that was with my not paying them.

WHY ARE WE SO CHATTY ON THE RUN?

In chapter 1, we saw how the free-flowing creative thinking many of us experience on runs dries up almost as soon as we stop. You've probably noticed the same thing about conversation. After a couple of miles, even the most introverted runners can open up as if they're at happy hour, only to revert to guardedness as soon as their heart rate returns to normal.

"I've been running with my running buddy for seven years, and we talk about everything, but because of our schedules, that's really the only time we're together," says clinical psychologist Laura Fredendall. "Then recently I saw her at the grocery store and was like, 'Oh, uh, hi . . . I like your shirt.'"

Although running can make you smarter in your sedentary hours, some cognitive skills diminish while you run. (Go ahead—see how much longer than usual it takes to do a complex math problem halfway into your next ten-miler.) Fredendall says that a similar temporary shift in the brain's activity might explain on-the-run logorrhea.

"Perhaps we're not as attuned to the part of the frontal lobe that manages judgment, anticipation of consequences, impulse control," she says. "So, maybe you're not worried about talking about your sex life with your running buddy."

There might be something to the happy hour analogy: "Having a couple beers can be like shutting down your prefrontal cortex," Fredendall says. "So, just like at a bar, on the run that part of the brain might not manage how you talk as much as other times."

Therapist Sepideh Saremi adds that concentrating on the effort of running might lessen the emotional intensity of otherwise tough subjects. "What happens for me is that things feel lighter," she says. "Even if you're talking about something difficult like your mother's cancer, you're not holding on to it or feeling it in the same way, because you're feeling a lot of other things in your body at the same time. It's almost like it distracts your body so that it makes it easier to tolerate talking about difficult things."

Saremi also thinks the logistics of running with others—looking ahead while side by side or single file—encourages more open conversations.

"There's something about not having the eye contact that makes us much more relaxed and comfortable," she says. "I hear from parents of teens that they get all the best information from kids in their car. Even with my friends from grad school, who are so open, it's when we went for walks or drove somewhere that I really got to know them. I think you feel less pressure talking about yourself when you don't have to look the person in the eye. There's a reason the priest doesn't look at you during confession."

PROFESSIONAL ON-THE-RUN TALK SESSIONS

Saremi has woven these insights on greater conversational openness into her work. In 2014, she started her private practice, Run Walk Talk, now located in Redondo Beach, California. After an initial in-office session, clients can opt to see Saremi while walking or running on an oceanside recreation path, two blocks from Saremi's office.

The genesis of Saremi's approach came in 2012, when she was working at a community health agency. "I had a lot of male clients," she says, "and it was hard for them to talk about emotional things or difficult things when they were sitting in an office with me and looking me in the eye. So, I went on walks with them, and I got so much more information. I think that was a function of being side by side and not having that sustained gaze."

Saremi assures her clients that the point of their mobile sessions is therapy, not a killer workout. They walk or run only as fast as is comfortable for the client to converse. Occasionally, Saremi is in the opposite situation, with a client whose conversational pace would be difficult for her. In those cases, "We talk about pace before we go out and that the point is to use the movement to check in with the body and understand what's happening in their lives. If they find the slower pace frustrating, we explore that," Saremi says. Before heading out, Saremi and her clients also discuss confidentiality issues stemming from being outside and what to do if they bump into a client's acquaintance.

Then they head out and back on the path, with Saremi setting a timer to mark the turnaround point. "We're doing the same things we'd do in an office," she says. "You're telling me about what's going on in your life." Saremi doesn't take notes during office sessions, so the inability to do so while running isn't a hindrance.

Saremi's clients include entrepreneurs and other driven professionals. She says that many of them value the walk or run therapy simply because they feel that combining a workout with therapy is more efficient use of their time. For others, however, being in motion allows for more effective sessions.

"Sometimes it makes the therapy possible," Saremi says. "They realize this feels good or that just being outside changes their mood. That might seem obvious, but when you're in the throes of depression or anxiety, it's really hard to believe that changing your environment or changing what you're doing with your body can change how you feel."

Saremi also takes what were originally office visits outside. "There have been sessions with people who are really depressed and get into really negative self-talk. I'll say, 'You're really in a bad place right now. I think we should go outside; walking might help.' And the thinking pattern changes. Movement and the scenery interrupts that negative flow." Fredendall likewise conducts mobile sessions when appropriate. "I keep my running shoes in the back room," she says. "With some patients I'll say, 'Let's go for a walk,' and we go out the back door and walk for a mile. It gets them started talking."

Sometimes Fredendall induces activity in her office. "I had a teenager who really struggles with depression," she says. "We took our pulse, we stood up, and we swung our arms back and forth, fake running for thirty seconds. We made a game out of it and kept going. She ended up smiling at the end of the session. For somebody who's really depressed, some sort of activation can be key to getting them to open up."

DIY ON-THE-RUN TALK SESSIONS

"For some people it's just a way into the relationship," Saremi says about her clients who are already runners. "The running is what allows them to feel safe" in being open with Saremi. Heather Johnson, who has anxiety, echoes Saremi on this count. "Though I may only see runner friends while running, I feel most at home with them," she says. "I feel safe." Combine that bond over a shared, valued activity with the chattiness that happens naturally on the run, and you've got the perfect setting for amateur talk therapy sessions.

"If you're finding that value in running with friends, then there is value in that for you," Saremi says. "It's not therapy, but it's certainly therapeutic." Fredendall is also a fan of non-therapy-professionals hashing things out on the run. "I think it has enormous benefits," she says. "In the 1950s women went to their hairdresser once a week. They really benefited from being able to talk to each other. Running with friends, you get that bonus of feeling good talking together, and so then you start associating running with something pleasant. When you're really depressed, that social aspect might be key to getting yourself to run and feeling better."

For many of us, conversation feels most natural when we're running. Part of that is because it's natural for the conversation to be no conversation. Long stretches of silence feel much more comfortable when you're running compared to talking with the same person while sitting or, even worse, on the phone. I recall with fondness an eleven-miler with a good friend in 1981 in which his "okay," indicating it was safe to cross a busy road, was the only word spoken in seventy-five minutes.

More common, of course, is the dialogue that starts three steps into a run with others and that ends only when you part. You might go from the weather, yesterday's tempo run, Netflix must-sees, and fears of death to the ubiquity of leaf blowers, shoe recommendations, spousal issues, and restaurant reviews, all in the first twenty minutes, before someone (usually me) breaks the conversational chain by making a pit stop. If you've regularly run with others, scattershot chats have probably helped you through days when you're more eager for the run to be over than you are interested in the experience of the run itself. For depressed or anxious runners, these meandering conversations can be a welcome break from the more worrisome topics that are often playing in our head.

What most of us find especially therapeutic are the in-depth talks that achieve at a minor level what professionals like Saremi and Fredendall provide. As with seeing a therapist, having to come up with the words to describe your problems forces you to better define exactly what's troubling you. And sometimes, that's all you want or need—a chance to vent, to articulate what's bothering you, and to feel that someone else understands you. That's how I've most benefited from oh-so-patient running partners. I'm usually not looking to them for solutions to such matters as fraying familial ties, the built-in sadness of knowing your pet will die in the next decade, or the dissatisfying difference in all creative projects between what you envision and what you produce. I just want to express aloud the thoughts that my mind plays whack-a-mole with in the middle of the night.

Other times you are looking for answers, or at least a sense of how someone else would approach a situation. One of my running partners, Meredith Anderson, says that running with others helps with her anxiety because she hears other perspectives: "People are asking me questions or they're not seeing things the same way I am. It's like a grounding, bringing me back from my tendency to let things spiral out of control. I think, 'Oh, that's how a normal person would look at this.'"

I've found that mobile talk therapy works best when running with one to three others. On larger group runs, it's natural for small packs to form and shift throughout the run. Sustained conversation with the same person or people the whole time is unlikely. The more people there are on the run, the greater the chance that someone is outside the circle of intimacy that a topic initiator might be comfortable with. With no more than a handful of close friends on the run, you know the boundaries and can talk more openly. The two runs are like the difference between joining colleagues at a bar after work and having coffee with a couple of close friends.

There's some self-efficacy involved in benefiting from run-talks with others. When I've been in regular therapy, I look forward to the sessions—it feels as if I'm doing something about my situation, even when it seems we talk about the same things week after week. I have the same anticipation of runs with good friends when I'm struggling mentally.

It's not that I head to the run planning to monopolize it with my woes, but there's a good chance at some point the Scott-finds-reality-disappointing topic will get some coverage. Just knowing that will occur makes things better.

For the first part of my running life, these conversations were almost entirely with men my age. When I could break 31:00 for 10K, the only people to train with were other young men. One of the great joys of getting older and slower (okay, maybe the only joy) has been an expanding pool of potential running partners. Over the last decade I've morphed into someone who runs almost entirely with women. I've also increasingly leaned on running with others as a form of talk therapy. Here's why the first development has greatly enhanced the effectiveness of the second.

Deborah Tannen is a linguist who is perhaps best known for her book *You Just Don't Understand: Women and Men in Conversation*. My key takeaway from reading the book (which I first read a quarter-century ago) was that men and women can have fundamentally different goals in conversation. According to Tannen, men approach conversation as an exchange of information; there's often an underlying competition to establish a pecking order when men talk. Tannen says that women see conversation more as a chance to bond; empathy, not one-upmanship, is usually the underlying ethos. These different approaches can lead to classic misunderstandings.

For example, Tannen says that if a woman describes a problem at work to her husband, he's likely to offer solutions.

The woman might then think the man isn't really listening to her. His hastily offered advice implies that her problem is easily solved, when what she really wants from the conversation is empathetic support. Conversely, Tannen says, if a man brings up a work problem with his wife, she might respond by relating a similar incident she's experienced. The man might then get frustrated because he's looking for a solution, but instead (he thinks) his wife has turned the conversation into one about her.

(A side note: Tannen describes how videos of boys talking to each other tend to show them side by side, looking ahead, whereas videos of girls conversing usually show them facing each other. This could be a way for boys to be more expressive than they would comfortably be when looking at each other. If so, it supports Saremi's idea that some of us might be more open with each other running because our gaze is mostly focused frontward.)

The gist is that running with women has helped me deal with depression much more than running with men used to do. I'm speaking on average here—I have a few longtime male running friends I can also talk with like this. But we see each other only once or twice a year. The conversations I have now with the women my wife calls "your girlfriends" have bolstered me through many difficult days. They've also laid the foundation for strong friendships that carry over into our sedentary hours. My life has been enriched by these relationships in a way that wasn't the case when I mostly valued training partners for help getting through tough workouts.

If you're fortunate to have running partners like mine, they might provide all the talk therapy you need for your depression or anxiety. It's not a knock on them if you need professional help. "Therapy is a very specific kind of relationship where the therapist is not getting their needs met at that time," Saremi says. "When you're with somebody who's not a therapist, you can't really expect that from them. It's more reciprocal—hopefully you take turns talking through things. There are certain responsibilities and interventions that a therapist has in mind and is doing that your running buddy is not."

Fredendall agrees. "The dialogue with others about what's occurring in our lives is extremely important," she says. "But sometimes what's needed is an objective observer saying, 'Are you still not feeling good? Is exercise not enough?' That therapy can add something to what you get from talking with your running friends."

"I don't have a problem when people say 'running is my therapy,'" Saremi says. "But I think that if you have something serious going on, maybe find a therapist as well. Clearly the talking is very helpful for you. If you're getting benefits while doing it with running partners, why not try it with a professional? You might get a little farther."

If you see a professional, one technique you might be encouraged to try is cognitive behavioral therapy. That's the subject of the next chapter.

CHAPTER 7

Running and Cognitive Behavioral Therapy

Imagine yourself in the final mile of a 5K. You've been operating near your aerobic maximum for the last several minutes. Maintaining a nice quick pop gets more difficult with each foot strike. Your chest feels as if a crate is slowly being lowered onto it.

Then, someone passes you. It's not a blow-by-you pass, but a gradual inching away. If you were watching the race on TV, you'd think, "The guy getting passed should tuck in behind her and get pulled to a faster time." But you're not watching the race, you're running it, and your immediate thought is, "I'm already maxed out. She's going faster than me. I can't keep up. Let her go."

Instantly you think about your immediate thoughts. Is it really true that you're maxed out and can't run even two seconds a mile faster? What about those times in workouts when you've pushed hard at the end and, instead of spontaneously combusting, ran faster? Why not try that now? Why not get in her slipstream and see how long you can stay with her? Won't you be happier for at least trying? Wouldn't you rather finish a few seconds faster?

In that fraction of a second, you decide your first thoughts weren't legitimate. You go with the other runner. Your agony level doesn't increase unbearably. You finish right behind her and wind up with your best 5K time of the year.

Without knowing it, you've just applied cognitive behavioral therapy (CBT), a common technique that mental-health therapists help people with depression or anxiety use to manage their internal dialogue and resulting actions. When running, especially when pushing ourselves, almost all of us have negative thoughts that run counter to our goals. But over time, we learn that simply having the thoughts doesn't mean we need to grant them legitimacy. We acknowledge them, examine them, and consider the consequences of following them. Usually, we set them aside and get back to the task at hand, because we know we'll be happier with ourselves later for seeing things through.

So, if, as runners with depression or anxiety, we wind up seeing a therapist who recommends CBT, we're already a few steps ahead. And we have another advantage: The CBT we instinctively practice as runners might also lead to greater pain tolerance and build a resilience that we can draw on in difficult nonrunning situations.

WHAT IS COGNITIVE BEHAVIORAL THERAPY?

CBT was created in the 1960s and formalized in the 1970s. It bridges traditional psychotherapy, focused on the feelings a person has, and behavioral therapy, focused on a person's actions. The bridge is CBT's emphasis on how thoughts (i.e., the "cognitive" part of CBT) lead to feelings, which lead to behaviors. In the above racing example, the initial thought "I'm already maxed out, I can't keep up with the runner who just passed me" might lead to feeling defeated, which might lead to not trying to match the other runner's pace. The second round of thoughts, such as "Just try tucking in and see how long you can get pulled along," might lead to feeling capable and newly inspired, which might lead to synching your stride with the other runner's and being able to increase your pace.

The goal of CBT is to produce behaviors that reduce rather than add to your problems, and thereby improve your feelings. One of its key insights is that self-defeating behaviors often stem from negative thoughts that seem to arrive automatically in the mind. For example, during a tough afternoon at work, someone with a drinking problem might immediately think, "I deserve a bottle of wine after this miserable day." CBT can help such a person recognize what's behind the thought (e.g., an unreasonable workload, a bad boss) and challenge both its validity and the proposed way to address it. CBT would help the person with the drinking problem see that, even if it's true that their workload and boss are to blame, getting drunk will not solve those problems, but will create others. The better choice in this situation, not drinking, will lead to feeling better about themselves. It might also lead to substitute behaviors, such as meditating or calling a friend, that will produce positive feelings such as calmness and being connected.

In its situational use, CBT is focused on short-term outcomes. Therapists help clients recognize the automatic thought patterns that lead to undesirable feelings and subsequent behaviors ("I can't go to work today because something disastrous is going to happen," "It doesn't matter what I do, so why bother getting out of bed?" and so on). Therapists then help clients devise and practice alternative strategies that, by leading to better actions, result in feeling better.

At the same time, CBT is a long-term technique, in that once you learn how to use it, it's available in any challenging setting for the rest of your life. Its viability outside a therapist's office makes CBT one of the most effective tools for improving symptoms in people with depression[1] and anxiety.[2] Some studies have found CBT to be as effective as antidepressants in treating mild to moderate depression. Research has also found that people using CBT instead of antidepressants have a much lower incidence of experiencing a new depressive episode.[3] Of course, a variable with CBT is the quality of therapy you receive. An excellent practitioner might better teach you to successfully practice CBT, whereas presumably a given antidepressant should affect you similarly regardless of what pharmacy you frequent.

Frank Brooks, PhD, is a professor of social work and strong advocate of CBT. He thinks that the specific change in thinking that occurs in CBT might have lasting effects on the brain. "Let's take obsessive-compulsive disorder," he says. "Sometimes medication is a successful treatment. What's happening there is probably an increase in neurotransmitters to that part of the brain that has control over [OCD]. But people have overcome [its] worst symptoms through CBT or other interventions that have nothing to do with neurotransmitters. So, how does that happen? Do CBT and other cognitive interventions reshape the brain, too? There's starting to be evidence that's true."

For example, one review of research looked at whether the brains of people with anxiety changed after they began using CBT, as determined by neuroimaging.[4] It did indeed find structural changes in the brain, specifically that CBT "modified the neural circuits involved in the regulation of negative emotions and fear extinction." These profound changes can happen relatively quickly. A Swedish study found that the part of the brain known as the amygdala shrank in people with social anxiety disorder after just nine weeks of internet-based CBT.[5] Activity in the amygdala decreased along with its size. In this case, brain shrinkage is good, because the amygdala is key to how we respond to and remember emotions, especially fear. These changes coincided with the people reporting significant improvement in their symptoms of social anxiety.

CBT and the structural changes it appears to produce are perhaps even more effective when combined with the brain changes brought about by exercise, such as increased circulation of neurotransmitters. That $1 + 1 = 3$ effect makes pairing CBT with exercise a go-to treatment for people with depression and anxiety. What's perhaps not as well appreciated is how being a runner primes us for success in using CBT.

THE RUNNER'S ADVANTAGE WITH CBT

I met Brooks as one of his clients. In one of our first sessions, as he started describing CBT, my thoughts drifted toward running. What Brooks was recommending as a cornerstone treatment for my depression and related issues was instantly familiar. It was the same cognitive process I'd used the previous three decades to counter such thoughts as "I can't hold this pace to the finish," "That fifth repeat was much harder than it should have been, I can't do three more," or "Another hour of running? That doesn't seem possible." When, years later, I told Brooks that I was able to meet our therapy goals because I told myself I already knew from running how to practice CBT, he said, "I think that's brilliant." (He is, as you would hope, a very supportive person.)

"What CBT teaches people to do is challenge automatic thoughts," Brooks says. "When you're running, you might have the thought 'I can't keep this up.' You very quickly go through the evidence whether that's true. Yes, you probably have some physical evidence that you're in pain. But then, you also counter that thought: 'Even though I feel this way, last time I did too, and I got through it. So, even though I feel this way, I can continue on.'"

As Brooks notes, the type of thinking we often use running is more sophisticated than repeating hackneyed mantras, such as "Pain is temporary, pride forever" or "The difference between champ and chump is you." It's a process of acknowledging unhelpful thoughts and then coming up with reasons that those thoughts aren't legitimate.

Brooks agrees that runners using CBT to address mental health issues could be at an advantage. "What people learn through CBT is that they can effectively challenge automatic negative thoughts. Most people don't know that when they start CBT. They think that thoughts are reality, that these thoughts are who and what we are, and that we don't really have any control over them. For people with high anxiety and deep depression, those thought patterns are really iron-clad: 'This is who I am and I can't change anything about it.' With your running, you already knew that's not the case. You already knew how to challenge those negative thoughts."

One of my running partners, Kristin Barry, says that CBT regularly practiced in running carries over into managing her depression. "Running has helped me to acknowledge a negative thought and then reframe it," the two-time Olympic Marathon Trials qualifier says. "When I was running well and I would have self-doubt, I would acknowledge the thought and then quickly counter it with something pre-planned of why I was ready to do X." When dealing with automatic thoughts that can prompt or worsen her depression, Barry says, "It's really just a different application of the same kind of thing."

Another of my running partners, Heather Johnson, specifically uses running to practice CBT, which helps her manage anxiety. "Training and incorporating tempos, intervals, and other hard efforts are great ways to combat negative self-talk, and accept and push through discomfort," she says. Indeed, our regular use of CBT while running may create a positive feedback loop of ever-greater ability to handle difficult situations.

RUNNERS REALLY ARE TOUGHER

Research backs what we like to believe about ourselves: Runners and other endurance athletes are tougher than sedentary people. Studies have found that we're better at holding up to and managing pain. Experts believe these attributes are more the result of our training and racing than inherent traits.

First, some terminology. Research on pain distinguishes between pain threshold and pain tolerance. *Pain threshold* is when you first describe a situation as painful. *Pain tolerance* is how long you tolerate the painful situation before giving up. (If only life were like research—in pain studies, the subjects can terminate the painful stimulus whenever they want.) Where we runners have the advantage is pain tolerance.

So, for example, Israeli researchers applied heat to subjects' arms to measure pain threshold (when the heat becomes painful) and pain tolerance (how long the subjects could tolerate the heat once they found it painful). The subjects were nineteen triathletes and seventeen nonathletes. The key takeaways were that the triathletes had much greater pain tolerance, they described the pain as less intense, and they didn't fear the pain as much as the sedentary subjects.[6] Similarly, a German study had ultramarathon runners and sedentary people stick their hand in a bucket of ice water for three minutes.[7] All eleven of the ultrarunners kept their hand in the bucket for the stipulated time, even though they thought it was painful. (On average, they rated that pain as a 6 out of 10.) A control group of eleven otherwise similar people who weren't ultrarunners fared much worse. Only three of them kept their hand in the bucket for three minutes; their average time was ninety-six seconds, or just more than half the duration they were encouraged to stick it out for. When the going got tough, the sedentary got going—in the direction of avoiding pain.

These findings, however, raise a chicken-or-egg question: Do some of the people do well as athletes because they naturally have a greater pain tolerance, or does being an athlete lead to developing greater pain tolerance? An Australian study circumvented that issue by measuring pain threshold and pain tolerance in a group of nonathletes, and then turning half of them into athletes and remeasuring pain threshold and pain tolerance after six weeks of training.[8]

The result? On one test, the people who trained increased their pain tolerance by 20 percent, while their pain threshold didn't change. They found a given sensation as painful as before but could handle that level of discomfort for significantly longer. The nonathletes were as relatively wimpy or tough as during the first round of testing.

It didn't take much training to apparently produce such a dramatic increase in pain tolerance. The people who became exercisers rode a stationary bike three times a week, for thirty minutes at a time, at a moderate intensity. It's worth noting that the mode of exercise was aerobic. The Israeli researchers who examined triathletes have tested the pain sensitivity of athletes in nonaerobic sports, such as power lifting, and found they score roughly the same as sedentary people.

It's also worth noting that some of the pain-tolerance tests were done on the participants' arms. The pain-tolerance test in question consisted of withstanding a tourniquet that decreased blood flow (and increased pain). Cycling, of course, doesn't specifically target arm muscles, so the increase in pain tolerance couldn't be attributed to the exercisers' becoming used to discomfort there. "This result provides evidence for a central mechanism as the primary modulator of the increased pain tolerance and suggests a new, psychological adaptation to training," the researchers note.

Although the new exercisers rode at a moderate intensity, they were beginners; for them, three half-hour workouts a week presumably counted as hard work. For regular runners, gains in toughness might be analogous to gains in racing fitness—basic, getting-in-the-miles training will get you far, but adding intensity will get you farther. A British study found that people who did high-intensity cycling workouts for six weeks improved their pain tolerance at the end of that time more than did people who did only moderate-intensity cycling.[9] "Every time you do the hard thing, the brain benefits," says clinical psychologist Laura Fredendall.

Getting fit can make you tougher, and getting tougher might also help you get that much more fit, the researchers speculate. In their words, "Exercise training may facilitate the development of brain function that increases tolerance of these signals and associated sensations, and this increase in tolerance may contribute to improved endurance performance."

When I described these athletes-are-tougher studies to Brooks, he said they made sense from his professional perspective. "The cognitive part of that is that you're able to challenge that automatic first thought of 'I can't do this.' You have daily experience of challenging those thoughts and not automatically granting them validity."

TAPPING YOUR TOUGHNESS

Research that compliments endurance athletes on our toughness comes with a caveat: We might be just as wimpy as everyone else when we're under acute psychological stress.

In a subsequent study, the original triathletes-are-toughies researchers again measured pain threshold and pain tolerance in a group of triathletes.[10] And not just any old triathletes, but highly ambitious ones who trained an average of sixteen hours a week and raced an average of twelve times a year. The triathletes told the researchers they regularly experienced moderate to high levels of physical and mental stress in training and competition. If anyone had gained real-life resilience from their athletic pursuits, these triathletes were good candidates.

This time, the triathletes underwent the pain tests before and during a common psychological test designed to induce stress. The researchers gathered not only the triathletes' subjective reports of stress, but also measured levels of cortisol, a stress hormone, in the triathletes' saliva.

The psychological test, called the Montreal Imaging Stress Task, is dastardly by design. For eight minutes, the triathletes were presented with arithmetic tasks on a computer screen. As they completed each one, the screen told them whether they'd answered correctly, and provided an ongoing tally of how they were doing compared to the average performance on the task. Before the test, the triathletes were told that the average person got 80 to 90 percent of the tasks right. That sounds stressful enough, but here's the cruel twist: The test was programmed so that, regardless of one's answers, the screen would always show a correct-response rate of 25 to 45 percent. To make things worse, after the first test, the subjects were told they'd done poorly, and that they'd have to do the test over. After the second test, the subjects were again told they'd performed well below average.

The main finding: During acute psychological stress—in this case, seeing and being told they were failing at a pressure-packed task—the triathletes' pain thresholds decreased significantly. In fact, their sensitivity to pain became essentially the same as that of the sedentary subjects in the earlier study. One of the researchers, Ruth Defrin, PhD, of Tel Aviv University, says that any event that's marked by unpredictability and that's not under your control could be stressful enough to have the effect found in her research.

There was at least one important way in which the triathletes remained different, namely, their willingness to see the stressful situation through to the end. Despite the stress-induced increased sensitivity to pain caused by the tests, the researchers wrote, "triathletes do persevere in extreme efforts even if these involve considerable pain and stress." Running—perhaps in part because it naturally makes us adept at practicing cognitive behavioral therapy—can give us applicable resilience in other areas of life. We know how to endure, even when hampered or hamstrung by depression or anxiety.

"When it comes to depression or anxiety-related problems, there's the idea that exercise builds hardiness," says J. Carson Smith, PhD, a brain researcher at the University of Maryland. Studies like the ones on triathletes' pain tolerance show that we athletes are better at dealing with stress in the moment. According to Smith, regularly experiencing unpleasant situations might improve your baseline ability to handle them, similar to how regular long runs make any one long run less of a stress. "Adapting to physical activity as a stressor may help you throughout life adapt to these stressors, not only in a physiological manner but also psychologically," he says.

I asked Defrin how runners can maintain their hard-won toughness in situations like the stressful ones she created in her research. "Techniques aimed to reduce stress, such as mindfulness, cognitive behavioral therapy, and social support, might have the potential to improve pain modulation," she says. We've seen that can be the case with CBT. In the next two chapters, we'll look at how to make mindfulness and strong social connections an integral part of your running, so that your weekly mileage can better help you manage depression or anxiety.

CHAPTER 8

Running and Mindfulness

Tempo runs weren't always Julia Lucas' favorite thing. When the former pro runner was a member of the Mammoth Track Club in California, she, like everyone on the team, did them weekly. Lucas was a five-thousand-meter specialist; eight-hundred-meter repeats on the track were more up her alley than forty minutes hard on the roads. On one particularly challenging tempo run, Lucas did what many of us would do—she repeatedly checked her watch. You can imagine the main line of thought: "Really, still twenty-eight minutes to go?"

Her coach, Terrence Mahon, was also not enjoying Lucas' tempo run, but for a different reason. After Lucas did one too many time checks, Mahon pulled alongside in a vehicle and yelled, "Stop looking at your damn watch and just run!"

Mahon's tone and wording are unlikely to be heard in your local meditation center. His overall message, however, might be. Mahon wanted Lucas to center herself in the present, to become engaged with the moment she found herself in. He wanted her to let go of regrets over the past ("Do I feel so bad because of what I ate last night?"), worries about the future ("How can I possibly do another twenty minutes, especially with that big hill coming up?"), and judgments about the present ("This sucks!"). He wanted her to just run. He wanted her to be mindful.

Running and mindfulness are linked in several ways. As Mahon was urging Lucas to do, having a present-only, judgment-free mind-set can lead to better performance. It can also lead to greater self-awareness, stress relief, and simple enjoyment of running. For fit and sedentary people alike, mindfulness has been shown to help with depression and anxiety. We runners with those conditions can draw on our running-related mindfulness experiences to improve our mental health at other times. We can also cultivate our mindful-running prowess to get that much more mental-health benefit from our runs.

WHAT IS MINDFULNESS?

You know something is popular when there's a backlash against it. Mindfulness has attained that dubious distinction, as evidenced by such jeremiads as the book *Mindlessness: The Corruption of Mindfulness in a Culture of Narcissism* and a *Washington Post* article "Mindfulness Would Be Good for You. If It Weren't So Selfish." The gist of the backlash is that mindfulness as popularly presented misrepresents true mindfulness. As the *Post* article puts it, "This ersatz version provides a vehicle for solipsism and an excuse for self-indulgence. It trumpets its own glories, promising health and spiritual purity with trendiness thrown in for the bargain." Mindfulness, these critics say, has become another it's-all-about-me phenomenon in an age of selfies, but that much worse because it comes with a veneer of virtue.

In the context of depression, anxiety, and running, mindfulness is best understood along the lines developed by Jon Kabat-Zinn, PhD, in the 1970s. A practitioner of Buddhist meditation, Kabat-Zinn peeled away the Eastern ontology to emphasize the practice's effectiveness in reducing stress and anxiety. In his 1994 book *Wherever You Go, There You Are: Mindfulness Meditation in Everyday Life*, Kabat-Zinn defines mindfulness as "the awareness that emerges through paying attention on purpose, in the present moment, and non-judgmentally to the unfolding of experience moment by moment."

Kabat-Zinn eventually codified his approach into an eight-week course known as Mindfulness-Based Stress Reduction. It and similar programs have two main components. First, purposefully observing your thoughts, feelings, and bodily sensations as they happen. Second, orienting yourself to present experience with acceptance rather than judgment.

As in cognitive behavioral therapy (CBT), the subject of the previous chapter, practitioners learn not to let their thoughts define them. In CBT, one goal is to challenge the validity of thoughts that can lead to undesirable behavior. Mindfulness encourages you to observe a thought without judgment; you accept it rather than challenge it. This different approach has worked its way into clinical practice. Frank Brooks, PhD, a clinical social worker, says that he increasingly uses acceptance and commitment therapy (ACT), which incorporates mindfulness, in his work. "ACT is all about teaching folks to use mindfulness and meditation techniques to accept right where they are at the present time," he says. "The commitment is to altering one's thought patterns so that they improve mood. CBT is almost all cognitive—cognitions lead to feelings, which lead to behaviors. ACT is more about being much more in touch with your mood and what's going on with you physically, which influences your thoughts."

There's solid evidence that mindfulness training à la the Kabat-Zinn approach helps people with depression or anxiety. A Dutch study found that people with a lifetime history of depression who learned to practice a mindfulness-based version of CBT experienced more moment-to-moment pleasant emotions and were better able to find pleasure in daily activities.[1] A review of studies looking at longer-term benefits of mindfulness concluded that the practice is a viable means of treatment for anxiety and depression.[2] Iranian researchers found that a mindfulness-based version of CBT was as effective as traditional CBT in reducing depressive symptoms.[3] A two-year study at the University of Oxford found that people who were trained in a mindfulness practice had no more relapse of depressive symptoms than people who took antidepressants.[4]

As with other forms of treatment, it's probable that adding regular exercise to mindfulness can make the practice that much more effective. A small study at Rutgers University tracked people with and without depression as they did an eight-week program combining mindfulness practice and exercise.[5] Twice a week, the participants did a seated twenty-minute mindfulness meditation, during which they were instructed to bring full attention to their breath. If they found themselves thinking about the past or future, they were to acknowledge this change in thought, and then return their attention to their breath. They then continued the meditation while walking slowly for ten minutes, which doubled as a warm-up for thirty minutes of running or cycling.

At the end of the study, both groups of participants reported fewer depressive symptoms; on average, the subjects with depression reported a 40 percent reduction in symptoms. The group with depression also said they had fewer ruminative thoughts, as they learned to use mindfulness to break the cycle of rutted thinking. Neural imaging found improved brain function in areas of the brain associated with cognitive control and conflict monitoring.

Taken together, these studies support runners with depression or anxiety experimenting with one of the many mindfulness programs now available. If you do, you'll probably find the practice isn't as exotic as it might seem. As a runner, you naturally experience a form of it all the time.

RUNNING IS FAR FROM MINDLESS

What do you think about when you run?

That question and "Aren't you worried about your knees?" must be the top results when you Google "how nonrunner should start conversation with runner." My usual answer of "Whatever" is meant to be concise, not curt. But it's perhaps confusing to nonrunners who haven't had the pleasure of being fit enough to cruise on autopilot for an hour watching yourself experiencing the world.

People have long been fascinated with what goes on in our mind when we run. Some of what's behind "What do you think about when you run?" is the belief that running is inherently a battle of mind over matter, where you have to will yourself to keep moving through either constant self-motivation or elaborate schemes to distract yourself. That belief underlies inquiries such as a 1983 research paper titled "Auto-Hypnosis in Long Distance Runners."[6] The author, Kenneth Callen, MD, surveyed more than four hundred runners on what they think about when they run. Callen reported, "Over half of the respondents experience a trance-like state with wide variation in depth, along with increased receptivity to internal events, absorption, and vivid visual imagery, all hallmarks of auto-hypnosis."

Callen's findings aren't as significant as his conclusion might make you believe. For one thing, he supplied the respondents with descriptions of this "trance-like state" and asked them whether they've experienced any while running. Examples include "sometimes form mental pictures while running" and "become more creative while running." To any longtime runner, these hardly seem like some mystical state, or, in Callen's words, "unaided hypnotic experiences which occur spontaneously." One of Callen's criteria was "have finished a run and been unable to recall everything which occurred during the run." By that standard, I enter "auto-hypnosis" when I grocery shop or shave.

I don't mean to beat up on a well-meaning inquirer from the first running boom. Much of this book is about how we think differently when we run. But one of the great appeals of running is that we don't consciously enact these cognitive processes; they just sort of happen. Within a mile of moderate running, our breathing naturally becomes rhythmic. The pleasantly repetitive cadence of our foot strikes can be felt in our head. (Recall what brain researcher J. Carson Smith said in chapter 4 about a nerve connection between the feet and brain.) As we settle in, we tend to exhale on a predictable per-foot strike schedule. Increased neural activity helps induce a free-flowing thought process. Running usually gets us part of the way toward mindfulness with little effort on our part.

Back to my "Whatever" answer to the "What do you think about when you run?" question: It's the most accurate description of what happens on easy runs, when the thoughts just come in and out from who knows where. Whether the weather will hold, a song you hadn't thought about for a decade, your right knee, your first pet, tomorrow's meeting, last year's vacation, whether you forgot your friend's birthday, your left hamstring, your right shoulder, the car that just passed too closely, whether you locked the house, and on and on and on, and that's all in the first half-mile.

"Letting my mind wander" is perhaps a more polite version of my "Whatever" response. Again, what's significant is that these observations of our body, mind, and environment in this present-oriented way occur with no real effort on our part. All that's needed to make the leap to mindfulness is to be nonjudgmental about them. My experience is that doing so is much easier while in motion than when sitting. That on-the-run practice then makes success at other times more likely.

A twist on this process is to choose an area of focus to reorient yourself if being nonjudgmental about your thought stream becomes overwhelming. This might take the form of repeating a phrase or mantra that will re-center you. As we'll see, focusing on a few key areas of running form, or your breathing, can also work. Phil Wharton, a renowned physiotherapist, told me he'll use a concept, such as the color green, as his mental lodestar. All these techniques can serve the same purpose as the clichéd monk's chant.

Perhaps I'm universalizing from my experience, but runners who are past their personal-record days might find mindful running easier. We have more practice in accepting our present running reality without judgment. (Or at least we should, unless we want to not fully enjoy the mental-health benefits of running for the next however many decades.) What is now my tempo run pace used to be my basic training pace. Accepting that development helps to cultivate the mind-set needed for mindfulness.

Regardless of where you're at in your running career, the temptation to constantly check splits is an affront to mindfulness. A training partner from my PR days once called out mile splits as we cooled down after a 10K race! Not surprisingly, he was an early adopter of GPS running watches. Perhaps the only benefit of my form of hearing loss is that I can't hear when my current running partners' watches beep to signal another mile has passed. Their wrist flick and quick glance down is a tip-off, though, that they're probably not participating in the unfolding present moment without judgment. Of course it helps to have a general sense of your fitness. But every mile on every run? What are you going to do with that information? As Terrence Mahon might say, stop looking at your damn watch and just run.

This is not to imply that mindful running is simply thinking, "I'm slow and that's okay." There's some evidence that mindfulness training as described earlier is indirectly or directly associated with improved performance. For example, two small studies of athletes found that a short period (four to eight weeks) of mindfulness training resulted in the athletes' subsequently scoring higher on measures of, well, mindfulness.[7] This might sound like research showing that four weeks of regular crossword puzzle practice makes people better at doing crosswords. Then again, some aspects of mindfulness, such as focusing your attention on your present task and accepting rather than worrying about bodily sensations, can improve performance. These findings aren't entirely dismissible on no-duh grounds.

More tantalizing is a follow-up to one of the two afore-mentioned studies.[8] In the original, researchers at Catholic University found that four weeks of mindfulness training improved mindfulness in the study's twenty-five runners compared to a control group of runners. But, they reported at the time, "no improvements in actual running performance were found." A year later, however, things were different. "The long-distance runners exhibited significant improvement in their mile times from pretest to follow-up, with significant correlations between change in runners' performance and trait variables," the researchers wrote. That is, the more the runners exhibited traits of mindfulness, such as not having what the researchers called "task-irrelevant thoughts," the more they improved over the year.

Of course, all sorts of factors can go into performance. For all we know, during that year, the more mindful runners started eating better or slept more or quit their job to do nothing but meditate and train. Still, if you heard a bunch of runners added an element to their training and improved more than runners who didn't add that element, you'd probably look into it, right?

MINDFUL RACING

There's another way in which mindfulness—or at least an aspect of it—can help you run faster. I think of it as converting form cues to mantras. It's a key takeaway from research on attentional focus, or what people concentrate on while running.

For years, runners have been told that there are two main coping strategies for the pain of racing—association and disassociation. The conventional wisdom was that association, or focusing on your body's reaction to the stress it's under, is what front-of-the-pack runners do, whereas disassociation, or thinking about other things to take your mind off your suffering, is what slower runners do. The usual take-home lesson was that if you care about performance, you should constantly monitor the feedback your body provides while racing.

Irish researchers have shown that things aren't that simple. In line with Terrence Mahon's intervention with Julia Lucas, they've found that thinking too much about how you're feeling can lead to running slower.[9]

The details of this research are complicated but worth delving into. The first step was to have twenty experienced runners do a three-kilometer self-paced time trial on a treadmill. That is, the runners controlled the pace of the treadmill and aimed to run 3K as fast as possible. Every four hundred meters, the runners indicated their rating of perceived exertion to the researchers. The runners' splits and heart rate were also recorded throughout.

The runners did two more treadmill 3K time trials. In one, with cues from the researchers, they tried to replicate the perceived exertion they had reported at regular intervals during the self-paced time trial. The runners controlled the treadmill's speed during this trial. (The treadmill's pace display was hidden to the runners; they simply could make the treadmill go faster or slower.)

In the other follow-up trial, the researchers controlled the treadmill's speed, which they matched to what the runners had selected at regular intervals in the self-paced trial. In other words, the runners ran the same splits in this trial as in the self-paced one, but the pace was externally controlled.

After all of the time trials, the researchers interviewed the runners about what they thought about during the runs. There were a few key differences in some of the variables measured among the three time-trial setups.

One significant result was that in the trial based on running by perceived exertion, the runners' 3K times were an average of 10 percent slower. For someone who usually runs 25:00 for a 5K race, finishing 10 percent slower means running 27:30, which for that person would usually be considered a bad race. The large difference occurred even though the slower run felt as hard as the faster ones (self-paced and externally paced).

Why might that have happened? The answer probably lies in differences in what the runners thought about during the three time trials.

During the perceived-exertion trial, the runners thought much less about specific aspects of running—pacing, improving their form, maintaining a good cadence—than during the other two trials. Instead, during the perceived-exertion trial, they thought a lot more about the more general notion of "effort/feel" than they did in the self-paced and externally paced trial.

But wait: Shouldn't we monitor ourselves while racing to make sure we're running at an effort level we can maintain to the finish? Isn't this what the association/disassociation model says elites do?

"If we focus too much on how we are feeling, then we are doing that at the expense of other attentional strategies that are beneficial to performance," lead researcher Noel Brick, PhD, told me via email. "Mental strategies like focusing on cadence, relaxing, technique, etc. can improve our pace without elevating our sense of effort. So check in periodically, do a body scan, see how everything is feeling. If everything feels good, focus back on those strategies that will help you run at your best."

Brick's advice is consistent with what many top runners say they think about while racing. After his unlikely victory at the 2014 Boston Marathon, Meb Keflezighi told me that in the last mile, when he was exhausted and his lead had shrunk to six seconds, he told himself, "Technique, technique, technique." When racing, Keflezighi internally repeats well-practiced form cues, such as "quick feet" or "relaxed shoulders." Doing so keeps him in the present and focuses his thoughts on something more specific than his overall fatigue, which might cause him to regret earlier race decisions or worry about the remaining miles. Brick calls this "task-appropriate focus of attention."

This form-cue-as-mantra technique has another big benefit: It should directly result in greater running efficiency, allowing you to run faster without increasing your perceived exertion. That approach is in line with the other key finding from Brick's study—on average, the runners' heart rate was 2 percent lower during the time trial when the researchers controlled the treadmill speed.

As a reminder, the researchers matched the treadmill's speed to the settings the runners had chosen in the self-paced time trial. So, the runners covered three kilometers in the same time in both settings, and with the same splits. But when the pace was set for the runners—even though it was the same pace they'd set for themselves—they completed the time trial at a slightly lower heart rate. This finding suggests that the runners could have completed the time trial faster if, for example, the researchers had let the runners set the pace for the final four hundred meters. Theoretically, the lower heart rate at the same pace should have given them the reserves to finish with a good kick.

"The 2 percent reduction in heart rate during the externally controlled pace trial was unexpected," Brick says. "But when we analyzed what the runners focused on—keeping relaxed and optimizing running action—then it made sense. We feel that the choice of mental strategy helped to improve movement economy, and this was reflected in the 2 percent reduction in heart rate."

Brick says this finding can have important practical applications. When the researchers controlled the pace, the runners didn't have to worry whether they were going too fast or too slow. Using form cues, they could focus on running as efficiently as possible at the given pace. "The externally controlled condition may be likened to running with a pace maker," Brick says. "If you are in a race with pace makers, use them. Let them do all the pace-related decision making. Instead, check periodically how you are feeling, and focus on keeping relaxed and running efficiently. If there are no pace makers, try to run with similar-ability runners. Maybe let this pack do your pace-setting, while you focus on keeping relaxed and efficient."

I don't want to come across as Mr. Anti-GPS, but it's important to note here that following an external pace maker is different from doing what you set your watch to do. Brick and other researchers believe constantly monitoring these devices is a poor "attentional strategy."

Christopher Fullerton, PhD, of the University of Kent in England, has investigated the intersection of psychology and pace. In *A Runner's Guide to Sports Psychology and Nutrition*, he writes, "Running with a GPS watch alone creates unnecessary anxiety around trying to religiously stick to a pre-determined pace that could be unrealistic, for example, if the weather changes. Tucking in at the beginning of the race or running with a group of runners could in fact be an effective strategy for decreasing the perception of effort required to sustain the pace you are trying to run."

Brick agrees, saying, "Our data backs this up—it might be better for runners to focus on strategies that will optimize performance and periodically check how they are feeling. I would suggest that constantly checking pace on a GPS device will distract from this process." After all, some of the strategies used by runners in Brick's study and elites like Keflezighi, such as relaxing tense body parts and focusing on good form, should lead to running more efficiently. The same can't be said for staring at your wrist and stressing that the last tenth of a mile was too slow.

Mindful running can also lead to a performance boost that can have nothing to do with faster times, but everything to do with the runs we all dream about.

GOING WITH THE FLOW

One of the main points of this book is that any run is better than no run for mental-health benefits. That's not to say all runs are equal. We've all had those precious day-of-days runs where everything clicks, where the barrier between you the runner and the run you're doing becomes porous, where you feel content and capable and would rather not be doing anything else. Kenneth Callen might call this auto-hypnosis. Mihaly Csikszentmihalyi has more famously and more accurately called this state "flow."

Csikszentmihalyi, a Hungarian psychologist, introduced the concept of flow in the 1970s. Driven by the belief that people are happiest when they experience flow, Csikszentmihalyi has worked to popularize the concept. Flow is often equated to "being in the zone," which helps with quick comprehension but doesn't delineate what he means. Here's Csikszentmihalyi himself, writing in his 2017 book *Running Flow*:

> In general, flow occurs when you believe you have the skills necessary to overcome a challenging situation. Your perception of time warps as your attention narrows to the task at hand. This attention is so sharply focused on the task that all extraneous thoughts and anxieties disappear. Clear goals drive your actions while all internal and external feedback verifies that the goal is achievable. Despite feeling invincible, you are aloof to what others think of you as your self-consciousness recedes into the background. All that matters is mastering the moment.[10]

Flow and mindfulness have much in common, including purposeful focus on the present; paying attention to mind, body, and environment; and a respite from regrets about the past and worries about the future. These are powerful payoffs for runners with depression or anxiety. With the sense of mastery it brings and its goal orientation, flow also produces strong feelings of self-efficacy.

A small 2011 study on athletes found another link.[11] Some of the subjects received mindfulness training twice a week for six weeks; the others didn't. At the end of the study, the mindfulness group reported significantly more frequent flow experiences than at the beginning, whereas the control group's frequency didn't change.

You may have been lucky enough to experience flow during a race. More often, it happens on daily runs, be they track workouts, easy trail runs, or medium-pace road runs. Csikszentmihalyi says that running in natural settings can make flow experiences more likely. That idea meshes well with what we saw in chapter 4 about greater mood improvements and more favorable brain chemistry when we do the same activity in nature versus human-made environments.

When I give running the attention it deserves, I experience flow a few times a month. It happens most often running on trails under a canopy of trees. I'm engaged but not overwhelmed by picking good footing. Peripherally I have a general impression of natural beauty. I navigate twists and turns, ups and downs as if I'm an extension of the trail. I wish I could stay in the forest forever. As morning light speckles my surroundings, I'm overcome with a sensation best articulated as simply "yes." Yes to the moment, yes to whatever is in store the rest of the day, yes to life itself. If I could bottle that feeling, I'd eventually forget what it's like to be depressed.

Running and Strong Social Connections

I wish "The Loneliness of the Long-Distance Runner" had never been written. Not because it's a bad short story—I wouldn't know; I haven't read it. It's the title that's bothersome. It's entered the general culture as a supposedly apt description of the runner's lot. Some of us cotton to it on our more martyrly runs.

Part of the problem stems from word connotation. The popular image of the solo runner assumes they're suffering from lack of company. But that's confusing being lonely with being alone. You've probably had many runs where you'd agree with Henry David Thoreau's contention that "I never found the companion that was so companionable as solitude." I sometimes feel most lonely in a crowd, thanks

to bombast-induced alienation and a yearning for in-depth conversation the situation is unlikely to allow.

The bigger issue is that being a runner more often means camaraderie than loneliness. Group track workouts, long runs with friends, postrace cooldowns with competitors—these and other bond-producing elements are part of the fabric of running. Even when you're running by yourself, you're aware that you're part of a worldwide web of fellow runners. You want lonely? Spend most of your waking hours flitting among social media feeds and working a job where more than small talk is rare, and not having an avocation like running that nurtures meaningful connections.

For runners with depression or anxiety, the social aspect of the sport might not seem to be primary to its appeal. Many of us are introverted and have no trouble logging most of our miles alone. Feeling connected to others, however, is often more a matter of quality than quantity. We're fortunate as runners to have a built-in way to forge the connections that can improve our mental health.

"I'M SO LONESOME I COULD CRY"

The relationship of loneliness to mental-health issues, especially depression, is well established.[1] The American Psychological Association lists social isolation as a risk factor for depression. Loneliness and depression can feed off each other, as a lack of energy or interest in activities keeps you homebound. Excusing yourself from social activities seems

easier than mounting the strength to smile and chat while you're miserable inside.

These feelings tend to compound with age. Old friends become dispersed, and their schedules harder to mesh with. Opportunities for making new friends narrow as a good chunk of most weeks is devoted to getting to, from, or being at work. Many new relationships seem to lack the depth of those from our earlier years. (It often feels that we gain acquaintances, not friends.) Dutch research on people over the age of sixty found that, over a two-year period, those who said they were lonely reported greater depressive symptoms at the end of the study.[2]

Animal studies have found a direct link between social isolation and less-favorable brain chemistry.[3] Researchers at the Massachusetts Institute of Technology measured levels of dopamine, a neurotransmitter linked to pleasure and reward, in the dorsal raphe nucleus area of the brain in mice. The dorsal raphe nucleus is involved in such physiological functions as learning, memory, and affect, or your emotional reaction to a stimulus (such as anger or euphoria).[4] Its greatest neurotransmitter is serotonin, which is partly why it's thought to be related to depression. In the study, the mice were isolated from one another, and then brought back together. Even after just twenty-four hours of isolation, when the mice were reunited, activity significantly increased in the dopamine-related neurons of the dorsal raphe nucleus. By simulating loneliness, the researchers appeared to show how brain health improves with social connections.

Of course, many of us feel more connected than ever, thanks to social media and other digital ways of staying in touch. But there's increasing evidence that these ties are no substitute for personal interaction. A now-famous study found that, over two weeks, the more people used Facebook, the worse they subsequently felt, and the more their satisfaction with their lives declined over time. These findings did not happen in regard to the subjects' direct social interactions. University of Pittsburgh researchers have found that, among young adults, the ones who spent the most time on social media had significantly higher odds of being depressed.[5] The same researchers found that those who spent two or more hours per day on social media were twice as likely to feel socially isolated than those who spent less than half an hour a day on social media.[6]

Humans evolved as social beings. Physical intimacy and satisfying interpersonal interactions result in elevated levels of oxytocin, a neurotransmitter that produces the warm glow associated with bonding. Even we introverts need regular in-person exposure to others; we just tend to feel those helpful connections in smaller circles of close associates compared to extraverts.

WITH RUNNING, JUST CONNECT

Enter running. As I said, it comes with a built-in way to create and strengthen just the sort of relationships that improve mental health. If, like me, you took up the sport as part of a school team, regularly training with others has been part of your running life since day one. If you're an adult-onset runner, you've probably nonetheless found benefit in having occasional company, especially for harder or longer workouts.

On any given day, runs with others provide a mood boost. "Running is often my favorite social hour," says one of my training partners, Heather Johnson, who runs in part to manage anxiety. Another, Kristin Barry, who has depression, says, "Socializing with friends while running makes me feel more connected and happier in general." (Just think if they got to run with someone more interesting than me!)

We saw in chapter 6 how training together often results in conversations that are more open and substantive than the norm in our sedentary hours. "Running with others has served as a way to bring my own struggles and achievements to others to gain alternative perspectives," Johnson says. "Over the years, social and group runs have given me new ways to approach parenting, working with others, and how to be a better overall person."

What's key here is that these more intimate conversations happen while we're doing something that in and of itself creates a connection. Runners know that you can learn more about a person in the space of a few ten-milers than in six months of having adjoining cubicles. The shared effort of a track workout or a long run builds a bond that's stronger than if we were in a book club or cooking class together. Combine the talk and the work, and you can build deep friendships in a surprisingly short time.

Running's delivery mechanism for a regular supply of new friends is a profound enough mental-health aid. In my fifties, I have an easy way to continue to broaden my pool of relationships at a time when many of my contemporaries are seeing their social circles shrink. Some running partners remain primarily that; when we encounter each other in what I call civilian life, we often do a double-take because of being unaccustomed to seeing each other in street clothes. (I often think, "There's a really thin person" before recognizing the other.) Some running partners blossom into all-hours friends who socialize while barely talking about running.

But there's more to it than just numbers. As Johnson says, "running has given me the opportunity to connect with so many different people." In the past year, I've run with people in their twenties and people in their seventies, as well as all ages between. Some are women, some are men. Some are married, some divorced, some never married. Some have grown children, some are childless, some have infants. Some began running as teens, some started recently. We grew up in different times and different places and spend our days doing different work. Our lives are so much richer for the varied friendships we continually develop through running. How else would it be the case that the best friend I've made in the past decade is a mother of two who was born after I started running? How many depressed men my age have a way to nurture such relationships in just one or two hours a week?

These too-brief in-person encounters don't exist in a vacuum. They spur actions and thoughts that improve the time

when we're apart. If you're like me, you're constantly checking in with your running partners: How did that workout
go? Is your leg feeling better? Want to go long this weekend?
Was it crazy cold this morning, or what? Running provides
an easy and obvious reason to stay in regular contact. As on
the run, the basic questions tend to lead to reports on nonrunning aspects of our lives, making our connections to one
another that much stronger. Even the most basic planning
to run with others helps. Knowing on a Wednesday that
Saturday morning will include ninety minutes of fellowship
brightens the week like little else. I used to plan to train
with others primarily as a means to a racing goal; now it's a
worthwhile goal in itself.

FINDING YOUR FRIENDS

Scheduling runs with others is standard advice for anyone
who struggles with consistency. You're more likely to stick
with a run if you know your friend is also getting up early and
will be waiting for you. This old trick has special pertinence
for runners with depression. As we saw in chapter 2, a key
way to lessen depressive symptoms is activation, or participating in enjoyable activities. Doing so breaks the downward
cycle of withdrawal, isolation, and lethargy. Committing to
meeting someone to run once or twice a week increases the
chances you'll get out the door on at least those days, and
those days can spur a positive feedback loop of more activity
and improved mood.

How best to find such people? New running partners can appear organically, as you run with one friend who brings along a friend, and you and the other person hit it off and start making running dates. More formally, you could explore regular runs put on by running clubs, stores, or other organizations.

Depending on how outgoing you are, try talking with people who finish right near you in a local race. You're probably well matched in terms of training pace, so if geography and logistics align, you could be set. Start by asking the person to join you on a post race cooldown. One of my best friendships started more than a quarter-century ago, when I said to the guy who'd finished one place ahead of me at a ten-miler, "Wanna go jog?"

An interesting side note: It turns out that the running tradition of the social cooldown might help you recover more quickly from a race or hard workout. This idea was popularized by University of Houston coach Steve Magness, who encourages his runners to jog together after a hard effort. Magness cites studies, such as one of rugby players,[7] that have found increased testosterone levels when athletes socialize rather than isolate themselves after competition. Time together can also be eating or having coffee soon after a draining run. A boost in your testosterone level is theoretically helpful because testosterone is among the hormones that speed recovery; have more of it circulating, and you'll bounce back from a track session, race, or long run faster.

You can usually tell after a few runs together whether someone's going to become a friend or remain an acquaintance. We all have different standards and needs. For many people, just having someone show up a couple days a week is a big help. But isn't it great when, on your third run together, you realize you're having the social highlight of your week, your mood has significantly improved, and you can't wait to plan the next run?

THE MANY MODES OF HELPFUL RUNNING GROUPS

My little anti-social-media screed doesn't mean there's no value in online running groups. They're most helpful when they supplement rather than replace in-person relationships.

When Pati Haaz was training for the New York City Marathon to climb out of depression caused by a miscarriage, she used a program provided by the race organizers, the New York Road Runners. (See the next chapter for more on how Haaz used marathon training to overcome a mental-health crisis.) Haaz felt she would benefit from additional support beyond the training program. The logistics of her life meant doing all of her running by herself, so she found another way to connect with fellow runners: She joined a Facebook group of people following the same program.

"These were people I didn't know in real life, but we all had the same goal," she says.

She felt accountable to the group, which helped when she was low on motivation. "We would share what we were doing, so I felt like I had to, especially on Sundays, when everybody would post about their long runs," Haaz says. "I wanted to share nice pictures from my long runs so instead of running my usual runs in the neighborhood I would get out a little farther and run in Princeton. Being in a pretty setting that was different from my normal life helped in itself."

During her marathon build-up, Haaz found that different social ties as well as different scenery helped decrease her depression. "Instead of dealing with the same people I was dealing with before [the miscarriage], I had the excuse to form a different group of relationships with people with the same goal as mine," she says. "Some of them became my best friends."

Another Facebook group has as its organizing principle not runners training for the same race, but runners battling depression. In 2017, Adam Weitz, of Orange County, California, created the group Sad Runner to complement his website of the same name. To Weitz, "Sad Runner" doesn't mean wallowing in one's depression. It means applying the mind-set of a runner to dealing with depression, such as tackling uphills (in running and life) rather than avoiding them and finding a way to keep moving forward.

The Facebook group, Weitz says, is "focused on positivity and action. So many depression groups are just places for people to complain about their condition. Our group focuses on motivating one another to keep going despite our [depression]. There aren't any victims in our group. We inspire one another to turn into fighters who live our lives no matter what depression throws at us."

One of the best unconventional groups I discovered is Run for It, a Canadian program that uses running to help girls aged twelve to nineteen learn about and address mental-health issues. Started in 2015, Run for It is now offered in seventeen Canadian cities. Participants meet twice a week for six weeks, with each meeting part training session and part lesson on mental health. The program culminates with participants running one of the 5Ks in Canada's Run for Women series. (Run for It is not to be confused with Girls on the Run, a US program for elementary- and middle school–age girls that uses prepping for a 5K as a way to build self-esteem and teach life skills, such as forming good relationships.)

Valerie Taylor, MD, the head psychiatrist at Women's College Hospital in Toronto, created the mental-health curriculum in consultation with other Canadian mental-health experts. The training program was developed by the Running Room, Canada's largest chain of running stores. Another popular Canadian chain, Shoppers Drug Mart, is also a sponsor, and the program has buy-in from local high schools and police departments. Taylor says the program plans to expand to include boys, at which time a curriculum appropriate for both sexes will be developed.

The goal of Run for It, Taylor says, is to raise awareness of and decrease the stigma associated with mental-health issues. In addition, she says, "we want to teach them about being proactive in their own health and engaging in physical activity, to augment medication or decrease the need for medication. One of the things we're trying to raise awareness of is that for symptoms of mild to moderate depression, you may not need medication, or if you have had more serious depression in the past and are still not feeling well, exercise can be a piece that helps you get back to the level of functioning you want."

The curriculum educates the girls on such topics as how running improves mental health, warning signs of mental-health problems, how to talk about a difficult subject (for example, mental health), and distinguishing good stress from bad stress. The short mental-health lessons end with discussion questions that the girls are encouraged to talk about during their training sessions, which immediately follow the lessons.

The creators of Run for It settled on running in part because it's accessible and known to be effective for mental-health issues in even small amounts. "There's a lot of misinformation out there about what exercise looks like," Taylor explains. "People are often told to do crazy things, like the Biggest Loser mentality—if you're going to start an exercise program, you have to go all out or it's not effective. For me, running is one of the least intimidating activities—you don't have to go to the gym, you don't have to be super rich or buy a lot of equipment or join a team. It's available to most people. You just have to follow a smart program."

The group aspect of the program is key to reinforcing its messages. "The girls run together, which helps to get them talking," Taylor says. "That helps break down stigma and make them feel more comfortable having conversations about some fairly challenging topics, like their mental health. I've seen people have conversations on the run that were very therapeutic that they'd probably otherwise never be able to have."

Although the 5K races the program culminates with also offer a one-kilometer walk, Taylor says almost all participants aim for the more ambitious running option. "The young girls felt like they wanted to challenge themselves and work toward a 5K run," she says. "Appropriate goal setting is really important, and I feel pretty strongly that unless they've got a serious injury, anybody can learn to run 5K over the course of a number of months if they do it properly and safely."

Goal setting isn't just important for teen girls aiming for their first 5K. It's a key part of using running to manage one's mental health, and the subject of the next chapter.

CHAPTER 10

Running and Meaningful Pursuits

When people find out you're a runner, one of the first questions they ask is some version of "How many miles a day do you run?" The question assumes that we all go out and do the same run day after day after day. It's part of the general perception of running as joyless castor oil consumption, an aerobic equivalent of flossing at bedtime and other things we do because we "should," not because we want to.

Most runners, of course, naturally mix things up. You run different courses, at different paces, depending on such variables as available time, energy level, previous days' workouts, weather, and whim. If you're like me, you usually give the well-meaning inquirer the answer to a slightly different question. "I do around sixty miles a week," I might reply. That sometimes leads to the other person saying, "That's eight miles a day." Depending on how patient the questioner appears and how pedantic I'm feeling, I'll say something like, "Well, it varies—some days I go longer than that, some days shorter."

I should know by now how to give people nice enough to ask about my running a brief answer and move on. Then again, they started it! I have this nagging mission to present running how I experience it, partially because I'd rather be ignored than misunderstood, and partially because more people might become runners if they knew the many ways it's wonderful. In my dream discussion, I convince the other person how running is one of the few things in life that can regularly give you something to work toward and look forward to in a personally meaningful way where the outcome is almost entirely based on you.

In his book *Why We Run*, renowned biologist and former champion ultramarathoner Bernd Heinrich writes, "We are psychologically evolved to pursue long-range goals, because through millions of years that is what we on average had to do in order to eat." According to Heinrich, hunter-gatherers had to persist in chasing down game despite the prey's often seeming out of reach. (Heinrich's original title for *Why We Run* was *Chasing the Antelope*, which he had to revise after threatened legal action by the author of *Run Like an Antelope*, a book about the jam band Phish.) The ancestral experience of working toward a challenging goal where success was neither guaranteed nor imminent permanently shaped human psychology, Heinrich says.

In this view, being fully human entails pursuing such quests, even—or perhaps especially—in an age of immediate gratification. When I visited him at his cabin in western Maine, Heinrich spoke about the need for "substitute chases" in modern life. Meaningful work or other projects, he believes, are essential for our mental health. That's especially the case for those of us with depression and anxiety, for whom the calendar can extend into infinity with nothing but dread or despondency in view. Fortunately, as runners, we have a built-in way to create substitute chases.

GIVING MEANING TO TIME

The sense that the unsatisfying present is your eternal fate is common during tough times. We can drown in such thoughts as, "I have nothing to look forward to" or "It doesn't matter what I do" or "It's always going to be like this." When you're struggling, you probably think like that about both life in general and your mental health, with the latter thoughts making the former ones worse.

Enter Heinrich's substitute chases, or what others more prosaically call good goals. By definition, they give you something to look forward to, and they directly contradict the perspective that, regardless of what you do, things are always going to be like they are right now.

Notice I wrote "good goals." For our purposes here, good goals have these elements:

Good goals are trackable. The nature of the goal gives you a built-in way to know objectively whether you met it. That aspect usually means you can easily set interim goals as you work toward your ultimate goal. So, for example, setting as a goal "finish a half marathon" meets this criterion, and would give you signposts to shoot for along the way (e.g., being able to run ten miles).

Good goals have a deadline. You should have a date by which you want to accomplish the goal. It should be far enough away to account for the work needed to achieve it (more on that in a bit) but near enough to bring a sense of urgency to your work toward it. Building on my example of a goal, if the longest you've run is six miles, then to "finish a half marathon three months from now" meets this criterion. You have time to build up your long run, but not so much time that it doesn't matter if you blow off running for two months.

Good goals require you to push yourself (within reason). If you run twelve miles every Saturday, then the goal "finish a half marathon three months from now" is pointless. You could accomplish it tomorrow. A good goal takes into account where you currently are and requires you to put in regular work to expand your capabilities. "It's gotta be difficult enough to make it challenging, interesting," Heinrich says. At the same time, it shouldn't be too ambitious. Your going from six miles to finishing a half marathon in three months will be challenging, but you should be able to meet your goal if you're diligent. If you instead set the goal "win a half marathon in three months," you're delusional. Good goals help you to change what reality is, but they can't be completely disconnected from reality.

Good goals are personally meaningful. This last point is crucial, especially if your goal in finding a good goal is to improve your mental health. A good goal is one that speaks to you, that you'll keep working toward when the work is hard because somewhere deep inside you want to attain it. It's something you really want to do to make life more interesting, enjoyable, and/or meaningful. If you, the would-be half-marathoner, set that goal because you think you "should" (to count as a "real runner," because it seems that everybody else is doing it, etc.), then you've let someone else set your goal.

It's no coincidence that I used a race to illustrate these elements of a good goal. They're the most obvious and readily available aspect of running for goal seekers. Running faster and/or farther than you ever have is one of the most intoxicating feelings available. A constant calendar of upcoming races to focus on has helped many depressed or anxious runners, including me for several years, lift themselves from the mire.

Races aren't the only available "substitute chase" for runners. After failing twice in the spring of 2000 to set a marathon personal best, I set the noncompetitive goal of running the 184-mile towpath of Maryland's C & O Canal in a week. Doing so entailed averaging just more than a marathon a day for seven days and covering 50 percent more miles in a week than I'd ever done. Those numbers didn't scare so much as motivate me—I wanted running the canal to be enjoyable rather than a grind. That meant I had to get fit enough to handle repeated days of long runs and disciplined enough between long runs to do all the recovery tricks that would have me ready to go again the next morning. It all worked. The week in November 2000 I spent cruising through nature for no better reason than to do so remains a life highlight.

Noncompetitive goals needn't be so extreme, of course. You might try to run every day for a month, or a season, or a year, or run more miles in a month than you ever have, or cover your favorite course ten seconds per mile faster than your best time on it. What's key is that your goal have the elements just described. That sort of quest will add meaning to your days and, as you see that you're not trapped in the eternal present, allow you to make progress in other areas of your life.

RUNNING TO RECOVERY

Pati Haaz is a perfect example of how working toward a running goal can be the catalyst for overcoming a mental health crisis.

In June 2015, the finance professional from Kendall Park, New Jersey, had a miscarriage while two months pregnant.

She became severely depressed and started missing work. "I didn't want to get out of bed, I didn't want to go out of my house," she says. "It was that feeling that there's no point in continuing. I had no motivation to do anything other than take care of my kids, which was more an automatic duty than the desire to do it." Guilt over being depressed—"feeling like I'm the worst mother in the world"—compounded the situation.

After a few weeks Haaz knew she needed to do something different, "at least for my children if not me." She started seeing a counselor, who asked her about hobbies and nonwork activities she enjoyed before the miscarriage. "The therapist told me, 'You have to continue doing those things even if you don't feel like it,'" Haaz says.

Haaz had secured an entry to that fall's New York City Marathon, her first attempt at the distance. When she became pregnant, she figured she would skip the race. After her miscarriage and the ensuing depression, "I just stayed with the assumption that I wasn't going to do it," she says. The therapist convinced her otherwise: "She said running even just a little would be good, but having this goal and pushing myself would really help me."

Haaz signed up for a virtual training program offered by the New York Road Runners, the race organizers. "I needed somebody to tell me exactly what to do," she says. "I didn't feel like I could get myself to do it on my own. I would get a daily email saying how far to run. It was easier for me to just follow their orders. Very, very often I didn't feel like waking up, but I'd look at my phone and see the email say, 'Today you have to run four miles in X amount of time.' That would get me out of bed and out there running."

Once on the roads, Haaz enjoyed the mobile change in thinking we looked at in earlier chapters: "I would start my run with all these negative thoughts, and somehow after one or one and a half miles, I was able to start thinking about something else—my pace, how much farther I had to go, any other thing." She also regularly reframed the thoughts that were keeping her depressed. "If I was driving or working or waking up in the middle of the night and thinking about the things that were making me sad, it would just make things worse. It would become like a spiral and there was no end to it," she says. "When I was running I would think about those same things but somehow I was able to process them differently. I realized the best time to process those thoughts was during runs."

The ambitious goal of running her first marathon wound up giving Haaz a significant boost in self-efficacy. "If I was running for the sake of running, I would have stopped with my six-mile run," she says. "I would have never tried to do sixteen, eighteen, twenty miles. I was accomplishing things I'd never done before. I'd never run farther than thirteen miles, and all of a sudden I was running at least thirteen miles every weekend. Pushing myself and seeing that I could keep going farther gave me satisfaction in other areas. I'm sure that helped me get better."

Haaz wound up finishing the marathon in 6:38, a huge accomplishment for someone who had been bedbound just months earlier. "I think running for the sake of running definitely helps, but it helped a lot more having this big goal," she says. "I joked with my therapist, 'One of the very first things you have to tell your patients is they have to go out and train for a marathon.'"

RUNNERS, WE'RE ALIKE

You might think that, because he's an elite runner whose livelihood depends on racing well, Rob Krar wouldn't get the same boost from a buildup that Haaz did. But he does, and counts it as central to managing his depression.

"When things are going well, there's almost like a synergy that works in a good way," says the two-time winner of the Western States Endurance Run, a hundred-miler in California that's considered the most prestigious ultramarathon in the United States. "I don't know if that's by coincidence or if internally some part of me deep down is able to recognize the importance of a big race."

Krar is subject to nearly incapacitating depressive episodes, but he almost never gets them soon before a major race. "I think it's the momentum and excitement leading up to it," he says. "If I can make it until a week or two before the race without crashing, it seems like the energy and anticipation is enough to carry me through."

Although Krar would prefer not to have mental-health problems, he does offer the intriguing thought that his prowess late in ultramarathons might stem in part because of his experience with depression.

When he's really struggling with depression, he sometimes sits by his door with his running shoes on, "and I'm just feeling powerless, literally not being able to step outside the door to run," he says. In his longest races, "the pain steadily increases through fifty, sixty, seventy miles, and you get to a point where you think, 'Wow, thirty more miles; how I am ever going to run thirty more miles?'" But rather than link that thought to his bad days at home, Krar reframes it.

"[The last miles of an ultra are] a long, hard struggle," he says. "Unlike on my worst days with depression, in the race I have the power to make the pain and suffering stop at any moment. I choose to continue to recognize it and work with it, and I'm okay with it. It's a unique time to be in a really dark place but be in control of it. It's comforting. I think that's what keeps me going back—to have that experience and have more control over it than I often do."

The goal-setting and process inherent in being a competitive runner are a big help to Rich Harfst in his lifelong struggle with depression. "Having consistent goals is therapeutic in two ways," the Annandale, Virginia, resident says. "First, the direct endorphin flow of going out and doing something—that often gets me over a hump. Second, things like writing a training schedule and tweaking it over and over and over again, or planning out races, or reading about and studying running, that systemic approach lets me apply consistent energy toward something which is also helpful to my mental health."

In his midfifties, Harfst is still aiming to get his marathon personal best below 3:00. He also finds purpose in other ways of tracking his performances, such as being competitive in his age group at local races or seeing how his times rate on age-grade tables, which attempt to compare times at common distances across age groups. (He also, and rightfully, draws meaning from "general comparison to my peers at work who are taking the elevator to take a cigarette break.")

For now, racing goals push Harfst to run more and harder than he otherwise would; the extra volume and intensity provide their own boost to his mental health. "That ability to measure results is highly motivating," he says. "On any given day, why run if I'm running just to be fit? There's not much of a difference toward that end if I run or don't run next Saturday. Without racing goals, I'd probably figure out another substitute for that, but the racing bit makes it pretty clean."

Rob Krar often suffers after he's achieved a big goal. "More times than not, I go into a postrace struggle like many people do," he says. "There's something about having been so focused for so long. When I do my best [in a race] tends to be when I fall the most following a race." Krar's experiences are a reminder to anticipate running's version of postpartum depression. Before completing your current goal, try to have a candidate or two ready for something you can focus on next. It needn't be as ambitious as your current goal, and it should probably be qualitatively different, perhaps in a non-running area of your life. But it should be something you'll find meaning in engaging with when you start to notice the glow fading from meeting your earlier goal.

VARIETY IS THE SPICE OF RUNNING

Haaz, Harfst, and Krar illustrate how focusing on a personally meaningful race can mitigate depression or anxiety. A less obvious aspect of preparing for a race can also provide relief. Its effects are significant enough that it's worth considering doing even if you have no current race goals.

Think back to the person at the beginning of this chapter who asked how many miles a day you run. When you're training for a race, odds are that a full answer would point out that not only do you vary distance by day, you also have different types of workouts. Say you're prepping for a half marathon. A typical week might include a long run on the weekend, a tempo run or workout of long intervals on one weekday, a day of shorter, faster repeats elsewhere in the work week, a steady distance run, and a couple of short, slow recovery runs. You might do some of these runs by yourself and some with one or more training partners. You might be on the track for the short, fast repeats, on trails for your long run, and on neighborhood roads for recovery runs.

Such a schedule will get you ready to race well, and looking ahead to the race is running's no-brainer version of a Bernd Heinrich substitute chase. Such a schedule will also be a daily antidote to the self-defeating idea that all your days are the same. Training to race gives your running a day-to-day purpose, a short-term version of the long-term focus a meaningful goal provides. You might feel that the rest of your life is a tire spinning deeper and deeper in a muddy rut, but you probably won't feel that way about your running when today you're running short and slow to recover from yesterday's interval workout, and tomorrow you'll be doing a steady eight-miler, and you have a weekend long run scheduled with friends to look forward to. The structure of training provides purpose to every day and the promise that tomorrow will be different.

Training to race can also boost your daily mood more than doing the same runs day after day. (Not that there's anything wrong with that!) We saw in chapter 4 that many runners report feeling happiest after their hardest and longest workouts. The sense of accomplishment that comes from knocking out a good tempo run before work or spending Saturday morning running farther than you have all year can stay with you all day. Seeing that, yes, you were able to overcome inertia and do this difficult thing, can inspire you to attempt other assaults on complacency.

Let's not discount the mental break that hard workouts and long runs can provide when your negative thoughts are stuck. "Long runs seem to be particularly helpful for me," my training partner Meredith Anderson says about temporary relief from her anxiety. "You're so tired doing this one thing that you don't have the space or capacity to worry about whatever's bothering you." For my part, hard sessions—tempo runs, intervals at 5K pace, short repeats at mile pace—are best at shunting my thoughts away from rumination on reality's shortcomings. Focusing on things like my split times, effort level, form, and breathing leaves room for little else. Of course, in one way, shifting my attention during that intense half hour doesn't solve the problem that bedraggled me preworkout; I still would benefit from feeling lonely less often, and so on. In another way, though, problem solved, if the main problem was the negative thinking the workout pushed aside.

A friend of mine used to tell his wife it was easier to run eighty miles a week than fifty. His counterintuitive reasoning was that being fit enough to average more than eleven miles a day meant that any given run took relatively less out of him. He could work very hard on individual days, but recover quickly, and be readier for more of the same the following day than was the case at lower mileage. My point here isn't that you should start doing eighty-mile weeks. It's that training to race—with runs of different lengths and intensity throughout the week—can provide that same extra oomph to your fitness level. You'll then be able to more regularly be on autopilot, cruising through your runs at the sustained intensity level most associated with running's feel-good effect. When I prepared for a trail ultramarathon in the spring of 2017, I got to where regular three-plus-hour runs became no more taxing than ninety minutes had been during the winter. The feeling of increased capability was with me on all runs once

I'd made the leap in fitness. That buildup was the happiest I'd been running in a few years.

TRAINING FOR NONRACERS

All that being the case, here's my suggestion for runners with depression or anxiety: Run as if you're training for a race, even when you're not.

When one of my training partners, Kristin Barry, temporarily put aside racing to concentrate on her legal career, she kept the structure that helped her qualify for two Olympic Marathon Trials. Her husband asked her why she was still doing track workouts early in the morning before going to work. "This is what I've been doing for twenty-five years," she told him. "It's the way I know how to run."

Barry and I discussed this topic over a run (for the record, an easy run, the day after both of us had done a hard workout despite having no races coming up). We agreed that continuing to structure our training as if we were preparing to race is a model that makes sense for us, especially as people with depression. We get the same day-to-day physical and mental variety that frequent racers do. Several different running experiences within a given week help distinguish that part of our lives from the all-the-days-are-the-same phenomenon that can initiate or worsen depressive thoughts. The big difference, of course, is that we're not building toward a race. We're sure to include substitute chases—a career milestone for Barry, writing a book for me—during these breaks from competition. Barry and I know we're going to run regularly anyway. It's easier, more enjoyable, and more beneficial for us to do so with every day being distinct but simultaneously related to other days.

A basic version of this approach to running will look familiar if you've followed many training programs. One day early in the week, usually Monday or Tuesday, I do a tempo run of twenty to thirty-five minutes at around half-marathon effort or longer intervals (four to six repeats of three to five minutes at 5K to 10K effort). Later in the week, I do shorter repeats (thirty seconds to one minute at mile effort). On the weekend I do my longest run of the week, usually between ninety minutes and two hours. Other days I go as far and fast (read: slow) as feels best given what I did the day before and what I have planned for the following day. (I stated my harder workouts in terms of effort, not pace, but I mostly do my faster runs by time on roads. If greater precision brings you more happiness, run their equivalents—eight-hundred-meter repeats, four-mile tempo runs, etc.—on the track or another calibrated course.)

Running as if you're training for a race even when you're not may seem weird. It certainly perplexes some fellow runners when they learn I run sixty miles a week, do hard workouts, and have no interest in how fast I can run a 10K. They might understand it better if they ran primarily to improve their mental health. One of the great appeals of running when I began as a teen was how it gave structure to my life. The one or two runs I did each day determined much of what

I did and didn't do in my nonrunning hours. The runs themselves—how far, how fast, how often—were somewhat dictated by my goals. Within each day, each week, each month, my activities cohered as building blocks to a better future.

At some point I started overthinking this way of thinking. Wasn't I just distracting myself from more important things? What does the universe care about my running? How is my running improving the world? Beyond times on a watch, how is my running improving me? Why do I give running so much meaning and energy when I so easily scoff at how others spend their time?

Now that I'm middle-aged, I find myself mostly back to my teen perspective. The main difference is that I often don't have a big race in mind, despite the impression my training log might give. I'm now completely comfortable with the idea that being a dedicated runner isn't a distraction; it's living. It's how I structure the most important substitute chase of all, that of outrunning depression.

CHAPTER 11

Running and
a Healthy Lifestyle

When people talk about "lifestyle interventions" to improve mental health, exercise is usually at the top of the list. So, we runners are fortunate enough to already have that important practice in place.

As runners, we know that getting in our miles is key, but that what we do when we're not running is also important. Elite runners talk about "the little things"—stretching, strengthening, form drills, diet, recovery, etc.—that add up to a big effect on their training and racing. The principle applies to those of us who use running to help manage depression or anxiety. Other lifestyle choices can have a significant effect on both our running and our mental health. In this chapter we'll look at several aspects of a healthy lifestyle, how they can help your mental health, and how being a runner can make success in implementing them more likely.

Improvements in your running or mental health after implementing these elements might be a placebo effect rooted in self-efficacy. But so what? If you feel better, you feel better. If that's a result of doing such things as eating well and sleeping better, at the least you're helping your overall health, independent of your mileage and mind.

DIET AND DEPRESSION

If you want the quickest route to argument with runners, don't ask about training methods or charity marathoners. Go with diet. You'll get responses ranging from every morsel need be painstakingly analyzed before it's consumed, because the athletic body is a temple, to nonchalance bordering on self-sabotage, on the theory that running absolves you from responsibility for all other lifestyle choices.

Most mainstream dietitians will tell you that the best diet for runners is the best diet for everybody—one high in fresh produce, lean proteins, and whole grains, with moderate amounts of unsaturated fat, and low on processed foods, fatty meats, and added sugar. Over time, many runners gravitate toward this general diet because it supports the energy level and health needed for good training, causes fewer gastrointestinal issues, and makes weight management easier than lots of fast food and packaged items with unpronounceable names.

As it turns out, there's evidence that the basic diet you might gravitate toward as a runner should help with depression. As Australian and New Zealand researchers put it in a 2017 study, "Although there are many versions of a 'healthful diet' in different countries and cultures, the available evidence from observational studies suggests that diets higher in plant foods, such as vegetables, fruits, legumes, and whole grains, and lean proteins, including fish, are associated with a reduced risk for depression, whilst dietary patterns that include more processed food and sugary products are associated with an increased risk of depression."[1] These associations appear to be independent of potentially intervening variables, such as socioeconomic status.

Of course, we all have our comfort foods, especially when our depression or anxiety is particularly strong. Mine is crunchy peanut butter straight out of the jar with a spoon. I'm not about denying myself pleasure—I figure the world does enough of that already. While indulging, I try to use this standard: What amount will lead to less overall time being depressed? Too little peanut butter is worse than none; I've teased myself with the prospect of short-term relief but provided none. Too much is worse than either too little or none, because I'll feel bloated and lethargic the rest of the day, including while running, and when repeated too often will lead to complaining to my wife about gaining weight. (My happy medium is nonetheless what most people would consider too much.)

Good diets call for real foods over supplements. A potential exception for depressed people is vitamin D in the winter, when limited ultraviolet B rays make it hard to meet your needs through sunlight. Vitamin D deficiency is associated with an increased risk of depression.[2] Getting the prescribed daily intake of 1,000 international units (IU) of vitamin D through diet alone is difficult, even with fortified foods. For example, a six-ounce salmon steak, which is one of the leading dietary sources of vitamin D, contains about 425 IUs. A large boiled egg, another top source of vitamin D, has about 260 IUs. The only dietary supplement I take is a daily 1,000 IU vitamin D pill, packaged as vitamin D3, in the winter. We'll look at another aspect of winter and vitamin D later in this chapter.

COFFEE AND CAFFEINE CONSUMPTION

Runners love their coffee. And for good reason—research has shown that caffeine can lower perceived exertion. That is, caffeine itself doesn't necessarily make you run faster, but it can make running a given pace feel easier, which in practical terms makes you more likely to keep that pace for longer. In long races, such as the marathon, coffee can help preserve some of your muscle glycogen (your body's form of stored carbohydrate) by increasing blood levels of free fatty acids, which can be used for fuel. This nice little trick can push the marathon's infamous Wall closer to the finish line. For more workaday runs, coffee is valued for increasing prerun alertness, which is always appreciated at 5:00 a.m. or after a long work day, and for moving things along the gastrointestinal tract. ("Don't leave the house until the coffee has left you," a professional marathoner once told me.)

Outside of running, coffee is believed to have health benefits. In studies comparing people who do and don't drink coffee, the coffee drinkers have been found to have less incidence of such diseases as type 2 diabetes, Alzheimer's, Parkinson's, and a few types of cancer.

So, you probably don't need me to convince you to drink coffee. For our purposes here, it's worth saying that runners with depression might be helping their mental health by being regular coffee drinkers. One review of research concluded that coffee consumption up to 400 milliliters (about 13.5 ounces) a day is associated with a lower risk of depression.[3] Another research review found that "the risk of depression decreased by 8 percent for each cup/day increment in coffee intake."[4] The latter review expressed the greatest benefits in milligrams of caffeine, not volume of coffee. "The risk of depression decreased faster and the association became significant when the caffeine consumption was above 68 mg/day and below 509 mg/day," the researchers wrote. By way of comparison, 16 ounces of Starbucks' Pike Place Roast contains 310 milligrams of caffeine.

As is true in much of the research on coffee and health, there appears to be some benefit for depression specific to coffee, not just caffeine. The first research review above also examined tea and caffeine consumption, and found the strongest association between drinking coffee and lowered depression risk. One possible explanation: Some research has found higher levels of baseline inflammation in people with depression.[5] Coffee (but not, say, a caffeine pill) contains antioxidants, which are thought to lower some forms of inflammation.

Note that the ranges cited in the research equate to moderate consumption. Ever more coffee won't help your mental health any more than it will your running. Even just a little too much can interfere with another lifestyle element that running can improve, and thereby help your mental health—sleep.

GETTING BETTER SLEEP

In surveys, as many as 90 percent of people with depression say they have sleep problems.[6] These problems often have to do with insufficient, poor-quality sleep (trouble falling asleep, waking frequently during the night, and/or waking for good earlier than desired). About 15 percent of people having a major depressive episode report hypersomnia—sleeping much more than usual and/or feeling sleepy most of the time they're awake. It's believed that bad sleep and depression are bidirectionally associated; that is, depression can detract from sleep quality, and poor sleep can worsen depression. The latter point is supported by reports of poor sleep by people before they have a depressive episode.[7]

Psychological aspects can compound the effects of poor sleep. Almost everyone knows the self-fulfilling drag of being wide awake and thinking, "Great, now I'm going to be exhausted tomorrow." More deleterious are the dark-night-of-the-soul thoughts that depressed or anxious people so often have. Everything that's wrong with your life feels even more wrong at 3:00 a.m. When dawn arrives, perhaps while you're on a run, you realize that things aren't as grim as they seemed. But the experience is draining. (I've often wondered why those witching-hour thoughts are always too dire. Why don't we ever lie awake thinking about how wonderful everything is, and then realize when the sun is up that our perceptions were overly rosy?)

Cecilia Bidwell considers adequate sleep, along with running, key to managing her anxiety. "I'm an eight-, nine-hours-a-day person," the attorney from Tampa says. "Here in Florida, I run super early in the summer because of the heat, and my Tuesday track group meets at five a.m., so those days I don't get as much sleep. But I'm pretty religious about going to bed early. One of the biggest triggers I have is getting even a little sleep-deprived."

By being a runner, Bidwell and the rest of us are increasing our chances of good sleep. Exercise results in sleep that lasts longer and is of higher quality (more time spent in restorative slow-wave sleep).[8] Check that: Regular exercise improves sleep. Research on people with insomnia who begin an exercise program has found that it can take three to four months of regular workouts for the sleep-better effect to kick in.[9] You've probably experienced acute incidents when running interferes with your sleep, via legs that are still twitching post-twenty-miler or a still-stimulated nervous system after an evening track workout. Those days are the exception. Being a regular runner should mean better sleep and greater relief from depression or anxiety.

LIGHT THERAPY FOR SEASONAL AFFECTIVE DISORDER

Having depression is one of the risk factors for the calendar-specific form of depression known as seasonal affective disorder (SAD). The far more common type of SAD occurs in the winter, and is marked by low energy, eating and sleeping too much, and withdrawing from social activities in favor of quasi-hibernation.

Obviously, it can be difficult to distinguish the symptoms of SAD from how a depressed person feels in May or August. Thanks to my running log, I've been able to notice patterns over the years as the seasons change. Where I live, the sun sets just after 4:00 p.m. during all of December. That month's entries are much more likely than any other month's to include such phrases as "beat again," "in a rut," "bagged group run," "no oomph," and "feeling chubby." I've noticed subtle improvements since I started using a light therapy box, which is thought to help by supplying in artificial form what the sun is skimping on that time of year. It's an unobtrusive enough process. Starting in early fall, I sit by the light almost immediately after getting out of bed, while having coffee, reading email, talking with my wife, and nudging our dog, who is at the lowest risk of depression of any mammal in history, out of the way. Twenty to thirty minutes a day like this is sufficient.

Light boxes don't emit ultraviolet B rays, the sun's vitamin D source. In addition to being triggered by altered circadian rhythms, it's believed that one reason depression worsens in the winter is lower vitamin D levels. In summer, between latitudes of 30 degrees north and 60 degrees north—from Houston to just south of Anchorage, Alaska—it takes only fifteen minutes of midday sun to provide about 80 percent of the recommended daily amount of vitamin D. In the winter, not only is there far less sunlight, but what sunlight there is transmits negligible amounts of ultraviolet B rays to the skin. In addition, many people are indoors for large chunks of the scant daylight time.

As runners, we have a regular opportunity to get some of that ultraviolet B light. Of course, during the shortest days of the year, fitting running into a normal work schedule often means starting and finishing runs in the dark. If possible, plan at least weekend runs for daylight hours. I try to do more morning runs in the winter; the 2:00 p.m. blahs when I haven't run yet are worse in January than July. Meeting others to run is especially helpful at that time of year in getting your butt out the door and forcing you to socialize.

RUNNING AND ALCOHOL

Alcohol is part of much of running culture, from postrace beer tents and winery-sponsored events to beer miles and rehydrating after a warm run with a cold pale ale. In Longmont, Colorado, you can swing by Shoes and Brews, a running store with more than twenty craft beers on tap to choose from after doing a group run from the shop. Shoes and Brews is emblematic of how the majority of runners can happily mix miles and mugs, with no significant adverse outcomes.

That's not necessarily the case for people with depression and anxiety. According to a National Institutes of Health report, depression and anxiety are significantly associated with substance abuse.[10] The report estimates that about 20 percent of people with a substance-use disorder have depression and/or anxiety, and that about 20 percent of people with depression and/or anxiety have a substance-abuse disorder. The report encourages medical professionals to consider mental health issues when treating people for substance abuse, and vice versa.

"So many people using substances are medicating themselves for anxiety or depression," says Frank Brooks, PhD, a therapist and clinical social worker in Portland, Maine. "They're trying to alter their mood. One of the reasons why it's so difficult to maintain sobriety over time is not because people don't have good intentions or don't know what to do, it's that they become overwhelmed by the anxiety or they slip into a depression, and self-medicate again."

Rehab programs often encourage people in recovery to run or do other exercise. In his book *Spark*, John Ratey, MD, writes, "As a treatment, exercise works from the top down in the brain, forcing addicts to adapt to a new stimulus and thereby allowing them to learn and appreciate alternative and healthy scenarios." Replacing drinking with running can be so effective that people who have done so quip about becoming addicted to running rather than alcohol.

She might not call herself addicted to running, but Heather Johnson is an example of someone who used running to help overcome substance abuse.

"I started running in 1998, the year that I stopped using alcohol as my crutch to manage anxiety and to dull panic attacks enough to live life," the South Portland, Maine, resident says. "During my first year as a recovering alcoholic, I had so much pent-up adrenaline, my head spun nonstop with thinking about drinking again, and I had to do something. I started walking daily, and when I couldn't walk fast and far enough, I started to run."

Johnson has remained sober for the last twenty years while running marathons, becoming a mother of three, and working in marketing. Whereas she used to turn to alcohol to manage her lifelong anxiety, now she runs. Being a runner not only provides Johnson relief, but gives her healthy practice in managing anxiety. "Running continually puts me in situations where I have to 'get through it,'" she says. "It's strange, but running probably puts me in more anxiety-provoking environments than anything else I do. It's constant practice to push through and accept the unknown. I'm sure it's created new neuropathways that have been intuitively applied to other areas of my life."

Running also helped Ryan Rathbun overcome a drinking problem. The Chicago resident says that he was a typical binge drinker in college—"nothing during the week, get all your school work done, then drink." He continued that pattern when he started working, "but then it started slowly creeping in a little more weeknights, having one or two drinks here, one or two there, and it got to the point where I was having four or five drinks every night and then still bingeing on the weekends." As we saw in chapter 5, Rathbun had occasionally been on antidepressants in high school and college, so he knew depression was a problem. But he disregarded it and the severity of his drinking. "I was in the mind-set of that's just me, that's what makes me cool.".

After an ultimatum from a romantic partner, Rathbun made big lifestyle changes, including resuming the running he'd done in high school and college. Running contributed to a concatenation of positivity—eating better, improved relationships, better self-image, weight loss—and he's succeeded for more than five years in leaving heavy drinking behind.

"I have a completely different relationship with alcohol," he says. "Now I can just have a glass of wine with dinner, or go out and have a drink or two at a bar. I don't worry about trying to keep it in control, because it just happens naturally."

Not all running-and-drinking stories are as straightforward.

THE OTHER SIDE OF RUNNING AND DRINKING

More than twenty years ago, a study out of the University of
Virginia and the Dean Medical Center found that runners
drank more than their nonrunning counterparts. On average, the male runners drank three to four times as many beers
per week than the male nonrunners. When researchers at the
University of Florida reviewed available studies on the topic,
they found that drinkers of all ages were more active than
nondrinking peers and that drinking and time spent working out increased together.[11] ("Findings were contrary to the
hypothesis of the investigators," the researchers admitted.)
A Penn State study found that positive correlation between
activity level and alcohol consumption exists on an individual level—the people tracked in the study drank more on
their workout days.[12]

According to Frank Brooks, about 10 percent of the
population will develop a substance abuse problem serious
enough to call for intervention. Combine that stat with the
aforementioned research, and you can see that the intersection of running and drinking can be different than Rathbun's
and Johnson's experiences.

Steve Kartalia of Westminster, Maryland, describes that
other possibility this way: "There were times when I would

drink too much the night before, but I'd figure, 'I still have it under control—I got up and ran twelve miles.'" That's the runner's version of heavy drinkers' self-delusion that they don't have a problem because they've never missed a day of work. As clinical psychologist Laura Fredendall notes, people at a high level in fields across society have problems with substance abuse. In some of those fields—creative endeavors, food service, sales—the underlying behavior is part of the culture. In other areas, including running, the correlation can be more puzzling. "Yes," was Brooks' one-word reply when I asked him whether he was surprised to treat serious runners for substance abuse.

But if you know enough running history, you can think of ways in which heavy drinking has been tolerated or even celebrated in running culture. I've already mentioned the beer tents, event sponsorship, and positive coverage of beer miles (which are essentially exercises in binge drinking and running). On the elite level, Frank Shorter famously enjoyed two liters of German beer the night before he won the 1972 Olympic Marathon. Former American record-holder Steve Prefontaine is widely believed to have been drunk when he fatally crashed his car in 1975. The ethos was best stated by 1972 Olympic medalist and 1983 New York City Marathon winner Rod Dixon when he said, "All I want to do is drink beer and train like an animal."

This isn't to say that Dixon or others from the era had a drinking problem (although former marathon world record-holder Steve Jones stopped drinking more than fifteen years ago, and is writing a book that will include details of his history with alcohol). Nor is it to ignore the multitudes of runners who drink in moderation and simply find beer to be a refreshing postworkout quaff.

What's significant is that, since at least the first running boom in the 1970s, alcohol's presence has been taken for granted in running publications and among runners. Kartalia was a high school and college runner in the 1980s, and went on to record personal bests of 28:32 for 10K and 2:18 for the marathon. He says, "It seemed like it was a highly respected, cool thing to be a hard drinker and also a badass on the track."

A British study offers some insight on why hard training and drinking immoderately might coexist. It found that people drink more when they've done something leading to ego depletion, or when your self-control resources are temporarily drained.[13] Ego depletion can occur after a trying mental or physical task. In running terms, it can be expressed as, "I used up a day's worth of mental capital getting through that track workout. Now it's Miller time." When you're running a hundred miles a week, including a hard session every few days, it's easy to feel that way more often than not. Also consider such research as a massive Dutch study on more than nineteen thousand twins and family members. Among its findings was that the regular exercisers scored higher on measures of "sensation seeking" (interest in new experiences, susceptibility to boredom, etc.), which has been linked to alcohol use.[14] At root, we runners aren't the grim Puritans many sedentary people take us for.

Another aspect of psychology might underlie heavy drinking in runners, and it points to why the behavior can often be seen at least as much in the front as in the back of the pack. Serious running attracts and rewards some of the same personality traits that can get you in trouble with alcohol: a more-is-better approach to things; the mind-set that if you're going to do something, then you should fully commit to it; and a tendency to explore boundaries rather than be content with good-enough. People who are the souls of moderation tend not to win races. "We wouldn't want to call that obsessive as much as an enthusiasm for pushing the limits," Fredendall says.

And then there's depression and anxiety. The either/or perspective of life as a drinker or life as a runner doesn't reflect many people's situations. Jokes about replacing one addiction with another ignore the possibility of a yes/and approach: Yes, some people want to get a certain feeling from running, and then they want to continue and compound that feeling with the help of alcohol.

Remember the stats about 20 percent of people with depression or anxiety having a substance abuse problem, and vice versa? According to Brooks, of the people he sees for help with substance abuse, almost all have underlying depression and/or anxiety. Is it so hard to believe that such people can simultaneously lean on running for relief from their mental health symptoms while also self-medicating with alcohol? "In terms of what the brain gets out of it, it's very similar," Fredendall says.

That was my experience for many years.

MY TIME AS A DRINKING RUNNER

I started running in 1979 as a ninth grader, a few months after I first got drunk. I have a distinct memory of two experiences from that time. First, splitting a quart of Schlitz Malt Liquor with my friend Bob, then standing in awe as an unfamiliar feeling of euphoria washed over me. Second, sitting on the porch after my first ten-miler, and noticing that the drained elation I felt was also something new, and welcome.

In chapter 4, I mentioned seminal psychologist William James' phrase "the Yes function." Here's the first part of that phrase used in context: "The sway of alcohol over mankind is unquestionably due to its power to stimulate the mystical faculties of human nature, usually crushed to earth by the cold facts and dry criticisms of the sober hour," James wrote. "Sobriety diminishes, discriminates, and says no; drunkenness expands, unites, and says yes. It is in fact the great exciter of the Yes function in man."

For a long time, that James quote described my relationship with alcohol. I was what you might consider an enthusiastic social drinker. I didn't drink most days, I didn't drink alone, I didn't stockpile drinks or plan drinking. Like most people, I could take it or leave it. But when I drank, boy, did I enjoy it. There were things I liked better about myself when under the influence: I was nicer, less sarcastic, more generous, more forgiving of others' foibles. Being buzzed was akin to how I felt running most days—a heightened sensory experience and a short, pleasant break from quotidian reality.

During that time, being a serious runner who enjoyed being drunk seldom caused problems. Occasionally I'd tell myself I'd make a good alcoholic—one of the more bizarre life goals one can set—because I never neglected school or work or running. In my sophomore year of college, I tied for first in a then-personal record at a half marathon while still loopy from the previous evening. The few times a year I got throw-up drunk, I'd have great runs the next day. I'd float along for ten to fifteen miles feeling light and cleaned out while thinking, "What kind of disincentive is this?" Following a late-afternoon track workout with beers—often without eating first, to hasten the buzz—resulted in feeling no different the next day than if I ate a good dinner and went to bed early. I was more or less indefatigable, and really fit from several years of seventy- to one hundred-mile weeks; drinking had no discernible effect on my recovery or progress. I continued to set PRs through my late twenties, some of which amazed me, like 51:01 for ten miles, or faster per mile than I'd run for two miles in high school. Many of my running friends had much the same relationship with alcohol, including an apparent lack of negative consequences.

But here's the conclusion of William James' quote: "It is part of the deeper mystery and tragedy of life that whiffs and gleams of something that we immediately recognize as excellent should be vouchsafed to so many of us only in the fleeting earlier phases of what in its totality is so degrading a poison."

At some point in my thirties I went from drinking when I felt good to drinking to feel better. An old album title by the band Spot 1019, *This World Owes Me a Buzz*, came to mind midafternoon most days. By then I'd been diagnosed with dysthymia and was usually taking an antidepressant. Intellectually, I knew regular consumption of a central nervous system depressant was among the worst things I could do for my mental health. But the pull of those former seemingly consequence-free times under the sway of the Yes function was so enticing.

That meant drinking more often, which of course meant needing to drink more for the same effect. When I began to notice others noticing my drinking, I more regularly drank liquor, for quicker effect, and I began to drink alone more often. Like Kartalia, I told myself I had my drinking under control, because I didn't miss runs or work.

I knew I was lying to myself. I would take do-you-have-a-drinking-problem quizzes online ("Have you ever felt that you should cut down on your drinking?" "Have people annoyed you by criticizing your drinking?") and pass (or fail, depending on how you look at it). I could always come up with a "yeah, but . . ." response to the questions. For example, people do a lot of things that annoy me. Why does that mean I'm in trouble with alcohol? But in moments of nondefensive honesty, I knew what the truth was.

As things continued to deteriorate, I began drinking secretly. I'd stash easily hidden, easily chugged 50-milliliter bottles of vodka in the attic or my clothes chest. When my wife realized this was happening, I hid liquor outside the house, often in spots I'd stop at in the last mile of a run. I was disgusted with myself, not just for how much time and men-tal energy I spent thinking about drinking, but even more so for regularly lying to and disappointing my wife. Things had obviously been heading in the wrong direction for a long time; the future looked even bleaker. The day before Thanksgiving 2008, I had my first session with Brooks. After several months that were harder than anything I'd ever done in running, I stopped drinking in the summer of 2009.

Being a runner in some ways went hand in hand with my drinking. Being a runner then became instrumental in quitting drinking.

Brooks recommended that I use cognitive behavioral therapy (CBT) to succeed on any given day in not drink-ing. For example, when the thought "This world owes me a buzz" popped up, I would examine it. What was behind that thought, and was it valid? Some days I'd tell myself, "Can the self-pity. You're healthy, you're married to the best person you're ever going to meet, you're not destitute and are unlikely ever to be, you don't have to work in an office, and there's ice cream in the freezer." Many days I'd decide, "Yes, you do deserve to feel better than you have the last several hours. But is alcohol the right way to meet that goal? The evidence is overwhelming that it's not. Even if you felt good after drinking, it would last for maybe twenty minutes. Drinking tonight doesn't hold up to cost-benefit analysis."

My main point in chapter 7 was that runners naturally use CBT all the time. We won't last long in the sport if we give up every time a run feels too far or too fast, or schedules and weather present challenges. Decades of experience in not granting thoughts immediate legitimacy made applying this technique to not drinking much easier than it otherwise would have been.

The second key way that running helped me stop drinking was that I milked the all-or-nothing mentality running can encourage for good, not ill. At first, I tried returning to light social drinking. That led to eternal internal questions: Is it okay to have a second beer? Is it too soon to have a glass of wine after having a beer four days ago? What happens if tomorrow we go to another party? Why am I really having this drink? Mulling these questions was far more trouble than any pleasure the drink provided. So, I switched my goal to living alcohol-free, and the mind-set needed to achieve that goal was instantly familiar. Decades ago I realized it's easier for me to run every day unless I'm injured or sick; I think about only when and where, not whether, to run. Applied to alcohol, that habit of mind means I don't waste any energy deciding if I'm going to drink today.

Finally, running has taught me how to navigate day-to-day difficulties while working toward a long-term goal. Running requires faith that your efforts are going to pay off, even though setbacks and futility are common. J. Carson Smith, PhD, a brain researcher at the University of Maryland, says that regular running should build psychological resilience along with a stronger brain. "You've been through a lot of situations where you had to push yourself and you've dealt with adversity, maybe even injury and recovery from injury, all these things that set you back," he says. "But you've been able to come through it and succeed or at least continue. Those times are hopefully life lessons that we take into tough situations."

When I first stopped drinking, I became more depressed than I'd been in a long time. Brooks told me my brain's reward system had more or less been given a bye for several years and needed to relearn how to work. I knew the severity of what I was experiencing was transient and that, like persevering through a difficult training period, I'd emerge on the other end stronger. In the meantime, I upped my mileage and ran with friends more often to get more of a daily mood boost. A big chocolate chip cookie at night also helped. After a few months, avoiding the temptation of alcohol became much easier, because I simply stopped thinking about drinking.

I wish I could report that my running improved dramatically once I stopped drinking. Other than not waking up dehydrated as often, I didn't notice much change. My life, however, improved immensely. Mostly, I feel liberated, now that the thoughts and behaviors that took up so much time and mental space aren't part of my existence. Meanwhile, most of the people I ran and drank with twenty years ago remain dedicated to both. All but Kartalia (who, incidentally, doesn't have depression or anxiety) declined to speak openly with me on the topic. But trust me that the ten-miles-in-the-morning, six-beers-at-night runner is very much a thing.

You may have reached your TMI limit pages ago. I

wanted to go into this level of detail for a few reasons. First, as my effort to destigmatize openness about problem drinking. Second, as a counterexample to the binary exercise-or-drugs rubric often heard. Finally, as a reminder that, while running is a powerful tool for managing your depression or anxiety, it's not necessarily a cure-all. That last notion—what running can and can't do for mental health—is the subject of the final chapter.

CHAPTER 12

What Running Can and Can't Do

Because we're going to save the world, my wife and I reuse the plastic bags we store produce in. Doing so entails rinsing the bags and then hanging them over the faucet to dry.

One night in February 2011 I was midway through bag rinsing when I suddenly stopped. I put my hands on the counter, lowered my head, and sighed, "I can't do this anymore." I slumped out of the kitchen to lie down on our bed.

As it turned out, the next day I had an appointment with my therapist. Frank Brooks and I were two years past overcoming my drinking problem but still seeing each other regularly about the root problem of depression. I started to relate my bag-rinsing crisis, and felt increasingly ridiculous the more I told the tale. I paused the narrative and said, "I

mean, it's not about the plastic bag, it's . . ." Brooks inter-
rupted and said, "Scott, it's never about the plastic bag."

Becoming overwhelmed by the environmental pointless-
ness of reusing this one plastic bag was akin to the cellular-level
sadness I felt in ninth grade reading about the twenty-four-
hour life cycle of mayflies. The mayfly incident confused me.
The bag incident inspired me. I now had enough experience
with depression to know it was a warning that things were
out of balance. At a time when I was writing a book while
working full-time, trying to get through the Maine winter,
and having your garden-variety middle-age existential crisis, sessions with Brooks and running with friends weren't
enough. Hearing "It's never about the plastic bag" prompted
a discussion that led to going back on antidepressants.

We've seen throughout this book the profound benefits
of running for people with depression or anxiety. My life
would be immeasurably worse if I'd not discovered it in 1979.
Sometimes, however, running's not enough. Like the spouse
who reminds you she's not responsible for your happiness,
running should be valued as a wellspring of support, not
something you outsource your well-being to. In this final
chapter, we'll look at how to keep running in perspective, and
how to know when you need more than running to manage
your mental health.

WHEN RUNNING'S NOT ENOUGH

Many people can adequately manage their depression or

anxiety primarily through running. In chapter 5, we met runners who, for a variety of reasons, have decided antidepressants aren't for them. Others forgo seeing a counselor because they feel they can keep their symptoms under adequate control without devoting time, money, and mental energy to regular therapy.

Cecilia Bidwell, an attorney from Tampa, hasn't ever received an official diagnosis for anxiety. After researching her symptoms, she discussed them with her gynecologist, who agreed that what Bidwell was describing sounded like anxiety. Bidwell refused the gynecologist's offer of a referral to a specialist. Before a minor medical procedure, Bidwell told the anesthetist she sometimes felt like her heart was racing. "He looked at my heart and said, 'You're in amazing shape, I wish everyone I put under were as fit as you. But I do think you have anxiety.'" Bidwell then discussed her symptoms with a friend who's a psychiatrist. "I said, 'If I don't run, I can't control it, but if I can get out and run for an hour, hour and a half every day and get enough sleep, I can keep things under control.'" Bidwell has remained resistant to other interventions. "This is something about who I am," she says about her standard mental state. "I don't want to dilute it. So long as I can run and sleep, I can handle it."

Rich Harfst, of Annandale, Virginia, has also landed on running as his main treatment. He's occasionally taken antidepressants or seen a counselor to address the depression that's been with him since he was a teen more than three decades ago. He didn't like the side effects from medication, including the weight gain that could interfere with being competitive in his age group. More broadly, "I don't want [being on medication] to become my norm—I want to have that safety net in case I go below my norm."

While in the army, Harfst didn't establish a long-term relationship with a therapist because he moved so frequently. "If I was in a new place I had to start all over with explaining my situation to a new doctor and going through the whole process from ground zero," he says. "That was frustrating to do, particularly if I was in a depressed state, so I just didn't do it." His wife, Jennifer, says that Harfst has another disincentive, even now that he's settled geographically: "There's a point to which it's beneficial, but then there's a point where it's the opposite of beneficial. It's throwing in his face the stuff that's making him depressed in the first place."

It's neither a failure of running nor the runner to consider additional treatment. "I have my own bias—I love running—but no, I wouldn't want to say that running is a cure for everything," says clinical psychologist Laura Fredendall. Just as a well-rounded training program includes elements that build on one another, some studies have found better outcomes when exercise is combined with medication and/or professional consultations.[1] Usually these studies involve people who are getting traditional therapy but are still significantly affected by depression or anxiety. Then some of the subjects start exercising regularly, and show improvements in symptoms and functioning in as few as six weeks. It's reasonable to think the reverse order—adding other treatments to an already-established running regimen—can be just as powerful.

Sepideh Saremi, a therapist who incorporates running into her practice, says, "I'm all about the lowest minimum dose. If the running works, do the running. But sometimes the running is not enough. When I was postpartum and really depressed and couldn't run, I did a lot of therapy. I still do therapy now even with being back to running. I'm for people getting what they need, and whatever that looks like, I think that's fine."

Deciding when running's not enough is usually a judgment call. Clinical psychiatrist and runner Brian Vasey says one key thing to evaluate is how well you're functioning in day-to-day life. "Are you able to do what you need to do and experience life to the depths that you would hope?" he says. "Are you experiencing joy and pleasure? Do you feel genuinely socially engaged? Are you feeling meaning in your life? Are you feeling like a contributing member of society and feeling good about that?"

Fredendall also says that quality of life is the best guide. "If running isn't enough, maybe your relationships aren't working, or you're still losing or gaining weight, or not sleeping, or not managing anger, or not performing in work or school," she says. "The dialogue with yourself or someone else about what's occurring in your life is so important. An objective observer can be extremely helpful, someone who can ask, 'Are you still not feeling good? Is exercise not enough?'"

Vasey acknowledges that making that judgment call of when to supplement your running can be challenging. "If someone's been dealing with anxiety or depression a long time, they may have developed ways of coping and managing so that they can function well enough," he says. Lifelong sufferers might not know any other way of navigating the world.

One key is a change in your functioning. When I had an existential crisis over rinsing a plastic bag, it was irrefutable evidence that something had shifted. What had worked for me the past few years—running, regular therapy, living alcohol-free—was no longer enough.

"If people are living life they're exposed to stress and loss and life events that are going to be difficult to manage," Vasey says. "That could lead to symptoms that, if they were to last more than a few weeks, would be diagnostic of a disorder. If I'm having problems with work and my mother just died and I'm not running because I have an injury, I'm not going to sleep as well, I'm going to be more irritable, and so on. If in the context of all these other things you're having these symptoms, it might be worth considering if you need extra help."

ARE YOU OVERLY RELIANT ON RUNNING?

One life event that might cause greater-than-normal symptoms is losing your linchpin—running—because of injury. It can be difficult bordering on impossible not to assume the worst. Sure, you've been hurt before and overcame it, but really, this time is different, the episode that will mark the end of the running career you've envisioned for yourself. Adding to the angst is that your usual main source of psychological well-being is now a major source of worry and woe.

All runners have these feelings when they're hurt, especially when the injury is bad enough to merit taking time off. A 2017 review of research on "exercise withdrawal" looked at what happened to people's mental health when they suddenly stopped working out.[2] (Yes, you read that right. These studies gathered a group of regular exercisers, and were able to convince half of them to voluntarily do no exercise, for anywhere from one to six weeks. A thought experiment: How much would you have to be paid to not exercise for six weeks?) The researchers found that the suddenly sedentary subjects consistently showed depressive symptoms, "including fatigue, tension, confusion, lower self-esteem, insomnia, and irritability," and an increase in general anxiety. The researchers also found that longer bouts of no workouts caused more of these symptoms in regular exercisers, with two weeks seeming to mark a threshold of significance.

Remember that these were people who voluntarily stopped exercising. Your reaction is likely to be even greater with injury, when ceasing to run isn't your choice. In addition, your withdrawal symptoms will probably be greater the more important you consider running to be to your wellbeing. A Brazilian study involving highly committed and more casual runners found that the first group had more depression, anger, and fatigue than the second group at the end of two weeks without exercise.[3]

How do you distinguish between injury blues that are acceptable and those that might indicate overreliance on running for your mental health? An example of the former is Fredendall's description of a lengthy bout with a hamstring injury. "I've never been depressed," she says, "but I did notice when I couldn't run for three months that my work became more difficult. I wasn't concentrating as well and I was feeling a little burnt out, even though I love my work." Contrast that with the blunt statement of Kristin Barry, who uses running to manage depression. "I am overly reliant on it," she says. "If I am unable to run due to injury, I sometimes am miserable. It's definitely not healthy."

If the feelings are so significant that they interfere with your life, you might be overly reliant on running to buttress your mental health, according to Brooks. "Ideally mood is pretty even across all situations and areas of functioning, including running," he says. "If something stops, you shouldn't plunge into a depression or feel more anxious. You might feel less fit and you might feel 'I really miss that,' but it shouldn't affect your mood so much that your functioning suffers significantly."

You might already have evidence whether you're leaning too much on running. According to Fredendall, training through injury because you're afraid of becoming depressed or anxious indicates that you're overly reliant on running to manage your mental health. "That would be a sign that there's something going on that's worth looking at," she says.

Amelia Gapin articulates that situation well. "For somebody who relies on running for mental health, when you're injured the first thing you think is, 'Oh no, how do I compensate for this now? And then it's not just that you're not running and don't have this thing that helps. You also have in your head, 'Now I'm not training, I'm further from my goal.' You get these new things that start feeding into the depression and anxiety and that makes it so much worse.

"I don't have a good way to handle that," Gapin says. "The worst part is that a lot of times it pushes me to run when I shouldn't—I either run through injury or I don't respect the early warning signs and tell myself I can run through this one. If I were smart or didn't have these other issues, it'd be easier to take two days off and keep something from getting worse."

Elite ultramarathoner Rob Krar also acknowledges that he sometimes pushes the injury envelope because of his reliance on running to help with depression. "I'm forty-one and been running for a long time, so I feel like I always have niggles or something going on I need to keep an eye on," he says. "It's important for me to feel good overall most days. I'm willing to take a little bit more of a risk for the sake of feeling good about myself even though I'm running through something somebody else might take time off for." Krar says that, over the years, he's mostly learned how to strike the right balance. "I'm now more aware of when I'm going over the line and when getting out for a run is only going to make things worse. My happiness can't depend solely on my running. Acknowledging that has been very important for me to help minimize the risk of injury and falling off-track in my training and racing."

A corollary to running through injury because you need the miles to manage your mood is running so much that your running suffers. Ali Nolan went through such a period between 2014 and 2016: "I was obsessive about running and thought the reason I was feeling so down, so anxious, so out of control was because I wasn't running hard or long enough. In the spring of 2016, when I was running twice a day because I couldn't stay focused on anything except running, I started to feel exhausted. I noticed that my coping mechanism might not be working. Running itself was becoming a source of compulsion and anxiety." While on vacation in Mexico, Nolan finally crashed. She began taking medication and reassessed her relationship with running. "Nowadays, I'm a lot more lax with my daily mileage and training plans. I use running when I need a break or to focus," she says.

KEEPING RUNNING IN PERSPECTIVE

Your running doesn't have to go off the rails for you to be overly reliant on it. The opposite can occur, where running goes so well that you practice a sort of willful ignorance about the rest of your life.

My late twenties were my fastest running years. I had always found setting personal bests to be highly motivating, much more so than racing for place. At my level at that time, where I finished in a race was mostly determined by who did—and more important, didn't—show up on a given day. Sometimes I won, sometimes I was twelfth, sometimes I was third. There were certain guys I was "supposed" to beat, but not because I'm by nature competitive or felt superior to them. They usually finished behind me, so unless I'd seen that they'd recently made a big leap forward, if they beat me it meant that I'd not run as close to my potential that day as I should have. An inherent need to conquer others just because we're engaged in the same pursuit isn't one of my defining personality traits.

But running faster than ever before? To me, that's captivating. Once I got my 10K PR into the 31:40s, I set the goal of breaking thirty-one minutes for the distance. In high school, my first big time goal had been to break 5:00 in the mile. Breaking thirty-one for 10K would mean doing so for 6.2 miles. I liked how the numbers of that comparison sounded as well as the thought of how my capabilities had increased in the decade since high school.

I knew to accomplish this goal I needed to up my mileage set point. Over several months I got to where I could regularly run one hundred miles a week and still have my twice-weekly hard workouts and weekend long run be of the same quality they'd been at seventy to eighty miles a week, which had been my norm the preceding several years. When, in the fall of 1991, I ran 30:57 at a 10K road race, I was my version of ecstatic, which is not so much fist-pumping and beaming as a quiet internal contentment over meeting a personally meaningful goal.

Putting in the work to break thirty-one minutes made me feel almost indefatigable when running. Usually I just sort of floated along at around 6:30 mile pace until it was time to stop. Running had always been a special time for me, but now the day's one or two runs often became the highlight. I felt a certain sense of mastery that was more satisfying than anything else in my life.

And that's where the warning should have come in. Ideally, the empowerment I got from running would have helped me in other parts of my life. When, as often was the case, work, relationships, or just general existence seemed pointless or stagnant, I should have been able to tell myself to stay hopeful and keep plugging away, because what had happened in my running could happen elsewhere.

Instead, I just ignored things. When I felt the familiar deflated yearning for a more satisfying life, I would tell myself, "Come on, you broke thirty-one minutes—how bad can things really be?" As a result, I was often miserable for most of my nonrunning hours, including when trying to sleep. And seeing lack of progress in other parts of my life mostly spurred me to focus that much more on running, the one area where I consistently felt capable of making the world like I wanted it to be. At work I'd think about where and how far to run come quitting time. On weekends I was happy to drive however far to run with others, because then

I wouldn't get home until noon, meaning less time to fill before my afternoon run.

The end of my runner's fantasy camp began on a high note, with a win in March 1993 at a prestigious local 20K. I decided to keep the positive momentum going and aim to surpass what was then the highest mileage week of my life, 123 miles. After six days, I had 108 miles. Unfortunately, also after six days, a freak mid-March blizzard hit the Washington, DC, area. I slipped and slid through a ridiculous eleven-miler in the morning, then an even more ridiculous six-miler in the evening to end the week with 125 miles. Instead of celebrating this accomplishment, I decided to surpass it the following week.

The next day, while doing two runs totaling twenty miles on slick roads, my right Achilles tendon started throbbing. The day after that, I couldn't run without limping and severe pain. In less than forty-eight hours I'd gone from the peak of my powers to immobility. As the zero-mile days continued I fell into a deep depression, compounded by my longtime girlfriend having recently dumped me. I recall lying on my bed watching melting blizzard snow flood my basement apartment and thinking, "That's a shame. Wish I cared enough to do something about it."

THE RIGHT RELATIONSHIP WITH RUNNING
I'd like to think I would handle that disappointment

differently now. Indeed, in 2013, I didn't run for five months before and after foot surgery, and kept functioning at an acceptable level. That's not because I care less about running than I did twenty-five years ago. If anything, I cherish running now more than ever. More time as a runner with depression means more clarity on how my marriage, friendships, work, physical health, and, of course, mental health are all so much better than they'd otherwise be if I didn't average an hour of running a day.

More time as a runner with depression has also allowed me to love running without smothering it. It's up to me—not running, not my wife, not work or novels or music or anything else—to cultivate the best Scott that's possible with the neurochemical hand I've been dealt.

As with any good relationship, that with running needs to be nurtured. The last time I failed significantly in that regard was at the beginning of the decade. For more than a year I tried to finesse my way through foot pain, mostly because I had taken on too much work and needed the stress relief I thought only running could provide. For reasons that make no sense to me now, I also decided to race a marathon for the first time in a dozen years. The 2012 Philadelphia Marathon became yet another second-half debacle. Running with zombie form the last several miles furthered the damage to my foot. But I wanted to capitalize on the fitness I'd squandered in the marathon, and tried to get back to normal training as soon as possible. Soon I was limping while running. Every day the state of my foot got me more depressed, so every day I headed out to run on it to temporarily abate that depression. By that January, things were so bad that I finally had the clarity to stop running.

After I had peroneal tendon surgery in April 2013, the orthopedist told me I'd never run more than twenty-five miles a week. This was a distressing prediction, given that I've averaged more than twice that since 1979. I didn't vow there and then in the recovery room to prove him wrong, but I was pretty sure his figure wasn't strongly backed by data. I hoped I'd be able to get back more toward that hour a day of running that elevates the other twenty-three hours.

Since then, my top running goal every year is "miss no days to injury." This is not the call to obsessiveness or ignoring my body it might sound like. I don't run if pain or tightness interferes with my normal stride. I've learned once and for all that's going to make prolonged injury more likely, especially now that my lifetime odometer is past 110,000 miles.

Instead, "miss no days to injury" is really code for "give back to running so that it can keep helping you." It's how I get myself to incorporate self-care into my daily routine. Stretching, strengthening, yoga, running form drills, not sitting for too long at once, eating well, staying at a good weight, not getting too exhausted—these all help me have a body that can hold up to the amount of running that supports my mental health. (Some of these areas of attention, such as diet and sleep, have their own depression-fighting benefits.) "Miss no days to injury" also means not taking unnecessary risks of too-sudden jumps in mileage or intensity. Yet it also entails regularly incorporating variety—in distance, speed, surface, shoes, and solo versus group runs—to combat physical and mental staleness.

This system has served me well. Since 2014, I've missed only a handful of days to injury. I've averaged close to sixty miles a week in that time and finished my first ultramarathon. More important, I've gotten running's unrivaled daily and cumulative help with managing lifelong depression, while feeling that the current state of my running is sustainable for many years to come. When, on March 1, I mark my running anniversary, I do so with fondness, recalling the many people I've run with, the running paths we've taken together, and the conversations and experiences we've shared. And I look ahead to more years of joint discoveries.

I hope that some of the ideas presented in this book help you find a similarly satisfying and therapeutic relationship with running. On your more difficult days, I hope that something you've read here helps you get out the door and make the day better than it otherwise would be. The key to feeling better is taking that first step.

APPENDIX: QUICK TIPS ON USING RUNNING TO MANAGE MENTAL HEALTH

Any run is better than no run when it comes to short-term mood improvement or long-term help with depression and anxiety. But some runs are more effective than others. Here's some brief guidance on how best to get a postrun boost. Most of these topics are covered in greater detail in chapter 4.

How Far: Most studies find significant mood boosts after 30 minutes of running. Improvements in mood tend to last longer after longer runs. But a 20-minute run is much closer to a 90-minute run than it is to not running. Avoid all-or-nothing thinking about duration or distance, such as that a "real" run has to be at least five miles long or it's not worth doing. The most important step on any day is the first one, the one that gets you out the door. On tough mental days, start your run with a flexible route that you can shorten or lengthen as feels best.

How Fast: Research has found the greatest increase in get-happy brain chemicals following moderate-intensity workouts. In running terms, that's your basic getting-in-the-miles effort at a conversational pace. But there's more to mood than brain chemical levels. Pushing yourself through a hard workout provides a needed sense of setting and accomplishing a goal. At the other end of the spectrum, give yourself permission to run as slowly as you want on especially tough mental days. Again, the most important thing about any one run is that it happens.

Where: People usually report better mood improvement (more tranquility, greater reduction in stress, anxiety, and depression) when running in natural settings compared with populated human-made environments. Of course, schedules and geography usually get in the way of regularly running through paradise. Choose visually interesting routes with minimal traffic as often as possible. When time allows, make an effort to run in beautiful settings for an above-and-beyond boost.

When: Plan to run whenever you're most likely to actually run most of the time. Many runners with depression and anxiety especially value morning runs because they set a positive tone and provide an example of success for the rest of the day.

With Whom: Assuming you have options on whether to run solo or with others, opt for whichever setup feels right for the day. Running by yourself can work best when you need to think through an issue with the help of that special on-the-run clarity. A solo run before or after a hectic day will probably also be more calming. Run with others when you need a break from your internal monologue or would benefit from talking through things with trusted friends. And if you're struggling to activate, schedule runs with others to increase the chances of getting out the door.

With What Purpose: Regularly mixing up all of the above variables should keep your running more interesting, which will make consistently going for runs more likely, which will mean greater mental-health benefits. Having runs of different length, intensity, and setting within each week also helps free you from the common thinking trap that all your days are the same.

Chapter 1: How Running Helps Your Brain

1. Paul T. Williams, "Walking and Running Are Associated with Similar Reductions in Cataract Risk," *Medicine & Science in Sports & Exercise* 45, no. 6 (June 2013): 1089–96, ncbi.nlm.nih.gov/pmc/articles/PMC3757559.

2. Fernando Gomez-Pinilla et al., "The Influence of Exercise on Cognitive Abilities," Comprehensive *Physiology* 3, no. 2 (January 2013): 403–28, ncbi.nlm.nih.gov/pmc/articles/PMC3951958.

3. Ryan S. Falk et al., "What Is the Association Between Sedentary Behaviour and Cognitive Function? A Systematic Review," *British Journal of Sports Medicine* 51, no. 10, bjsm.bmj.com/content/51/10/800?etoc.

4. P. J. Smith et al., "Aerobic Exercise and Neurocognitive Performance: A Meta-analytic Review of Randomized Controlled Trials," *Psychosomatic Medicine* 72, no. 3 (April 2010): 239–52, ncbi.nlm.nih.gov/pubmed/20223924.

5. A. Luque-Casado et al., "Differences in Sustained Attention Capacity as a Function of Aerobic Fitness," *Medicine & Science in Sports & Exercise* 48, no. 5 (May 2016): 887–95, ncbi.nlm.nih.gov/pubmed/26694844.

6. Benjamin A. Sibley et al., "The Relationship Between Physical Activity and Cognition in Children: A Meta-analysis," *Pediatric Exercise Science* 15, no. 3 (August 2003), journals.humankinetics.com/doi/abs/10.1123/pes.15.3.243; E. W. Griffin, et al., "Aerobic Exercise Improves Hippocampal Function and Increases BDNF in the Serum of Young Adult Males," *Physiology & Behavior* 104, no. 5 (October 24, 2011):

934–41, www.ncbi.nlm.nih.gov/pubmed/21722657; Takashi Tarumi et al., "Cerebral/Peripheral Vascular Reactivity and Neurocognition in Middle-Age Athletes," *Medicine and Science in Sports and Exercise* 47, no. 12 (December 2015): 2595–2603, ncbi.nlm.nih.gov/pmc/articles/PMC4644461; Stanley Colcombe et al., "Fitness Effects on the Cognitive Function of Older Adults," *Psychological Science* 14, no. 2 (2003), journals.sagepub.com/doi/10.1111/1467-9280.t01-1-01430.

7.   Lorenza S. Colzato et al., "The Impact of Physical Exercise on Convergent and Divergent Thinking," *Frontiers in Human Neuroscience* (December 2, 2013), frontiersin.org/articles/10.3389/fnhum.2013.00824/full.

8.   H. Tsukamoto et al., "Effect of Exercise Intensity and Duration on Postexercise Executive Function," *Medicine and Science in Sports and Exercise* 49, no. 4 (April 2017): 774–84, ncbi.nlm.nih.gov/pubmed/27846044.

9.   N. Zhu et al., "Cardiorespiratory Fitness and Cognitive Function in Middle Age: The CARDIA Study," *Neurology* 82, no. 15 (April 15, 2014): 1339–46, ncbi.nlm.nih.gov/pubmed/24696506.

10. Louis Bherer et al., "A Review of the Effects of Physical Activity and Exercise on Cognitive and Brain Functions in Older Adults," *Journal of Aging Research* (2013): 657508, ncbi.nlm.nih.gov/pmc/articles/PMC3786463.

11. Eric D. Vidoni et al., "Dose-Response of Aerobic Exercise on Cognition: A Community-Based, Pilot Randomized Controlled Trial," *PLoS One* (July 9, 2015), journals.plos.org/plosone/article?id=10.1371/journal.pone.0131647.

12. H. Y. Moon, et al., "Running-Induced Systemic Cathepsin B Secretion Is Associated with Memory Function," *Cell Metabolism* 4, no. 2 (August 9, 2016): 332–40, sciencedirect.com/science/article/pii/S1550413116302479.

13. David A. Raichlen, et al., "Differences in Resting State Functional Connectivity between Young Adult Endurance Athletes and Healthy Controls," *Frontiers in Human Neuroscience* (November 29, 2016), frontiersin.org/articles/10.3389/fnhum.2016.00610/full.

Chapter 2: How Running Helps People with Depression

1.   J. A. Blumenthal et al., "Exercise and Pharmacotherapy in the

Treatment of Major Depressive Disorder," *Psychosomatic Medicine* 69, no. 7 (September–October 2007): 587–96, ncbi.nlm.nih.gov/pubmed/17846259.

2. B. M. Hoffman, et al., "Exercise and Pharmacotherapy in Patients with Major Depression: One-Year Follow-Up of the SMILE Study," *Psychosomatic Medicine* 73, no. 2 (February–March 2011): 127–33, ncbi.nlm.nih.gov/pubmed/21148807.

3. Yael Netz, "Is the Comparison Between Exercise and Pharmacologic Treatment of Depression in the Clinical Practice Guideline of the American College of Physicians Evidence-Based?" *Frontiers in Pharmacology* (May 15, 2017), frontiersin.org/articles/10.3389/fphar.2017.00257/full.

4. Gary M. Cooney et al., "Exercise for Depression," Cochrane Library, September 12, 2013, onlinelibrary.wiley.com/doi/10.1002/14651858 .CD004366.pub6/full.

5. A. Pilu et al., "Efficacy of Physical Activity in the Adjunctive Treatment of Major Depressive Disorders: Preliminary Results," *Clinical Practice & Epidemiology in Mental Health* 3 (2007): 8, ncbi.nlm.nih.gov/pmc/articles/PMC1976311.

6. Samuel B. Harvey et al., "Exercise and the Prevention of Depression: Results of the HUNT Cohort Study," *American Journal of Psychiatry* (October 3, 2017), ajp.psychiatryonline.org/doi/abs/10.1176/appi .ajp.2017.16111223.

7. L. Zhai et al., "Sedentary Behavior and the Risk of Depression: A Meta-analysis," *British Journal of Sports Medicine* 49, no. 11, bjsm.bmj.com/content/49/11/705.

8. T. W. Lin et al., "Exercise Benefits Brain Function: The Monoamine Connection," *Brain Sciences* 3, no. 1 (March 2013): 39–53, ncbi.nlm .nih.gov/pubmed/24961306; J. Gourgouvelis et al., "Exercise Promotes Neuroplasticity in Both Healthy and Depressed Brains: An fMRI Pilot Study," *Neural Plasticity* 2017, hindawi.com/journals/np/2017/8305287.

9. Devin K. Binder et al., "Brain-Derived Neurotrophic Factor," *Growth Factors* 22, no. 2 (September 2004): 123–31, ncbi.nlm.nih.gov/pmc/articles/PMC2504526.

10. T. Huang et al., "The Effects of Physical Activity and Exercise on Brain-Derived Neurotrophic Factor in Healthy Humans: A Review,"

Scandinavian Journal of Medicine and Science in Sports 24, no. 1 (February 2014): 1–10, ncbi.nlm.nih.gov/pubmed/23600729.

11. K. L. Szuhany et al., "A Meta-analytic Review of the Effects of Exercise on Brain-Derived Neurotrophic Factor," *Journal of Psychiatric Research* 60 (January 2015): 56–64, ncbi.nlm.nih.gov/pubmed/25455510. ncbi.nlm.nih.gov/pubmed/23600729.

12. P. Salmon, "Effects of Physical Exercise on Anxiety, Depression, and Sensitivity to Stress: A Unifying Theory," *Clinical Psychology Review* 21, no. 1 (February 2001): 33–61, ncbi.nlm.nih.gov/pubmed/11148895.

Chapter 3: How Running Helps People with Anxiety

1. R. C. Kessler et al., "Lifetime Prevalence and Age-of-Onset Distributions of DSM-IV Disorders in the National Comorbidity Survey Replication," *Archives of General Psychiatry* 62, no. 6 (June 2005): 593–602, ncbi.nlm.nih.gov/pubmed/15939837.

2. R. D. Goodwin, "Association Between Physical Activity and Mental Disorders Among Adults in the United States," *Preventive Medicine* 36, no. 6 (June 2003): 698–703, ncbi.nlm.nih.gov/pubmed/12744913; M. H. De Moor, et al., "Regular Exercise, Anxiety, Depression and Personality: A Population-Based Study," *Preventive Medicine* 42, no. 4 (April 2006): 273–79, ncbi.nlm.nih.gov/pubmed/16439008.

3. S. J. Petruzzelo et al., "A Meta-analysis on the Anxiety-Reducing Effects of Acute and Chronic Exercise. Outcomes and Mechanisms," *Sports Medicine* 11, no. 3 (March 1991): 143–82, ncbi.nlm.nih.gov/pubmed/1828608.

4. Matthew P. Herring et al., "The Effect of Exercise Training on Anxiety Symptoms Among Patients. A Systematic Review," *Archives of Internal Medicine* 170, no. 4 (2010): 321–31, jamanetwork.com/journals/jamainternalmedicine/fullarticle/774421.

5. Brendon Stubbs et al., "An Examination of the Anxiolytic Effects of Exercise for People with Anxiety and Stress-Related Disorders: A Meta-analysis," *Psychiatry Research* 249 (March 2017): 102–8, psy-journal.com/article/S0165-1781(16)30909-X/abstract.

6. Gregory L. Stonerock et al., "Exercise as Treatment for Anxiety: Systematic Review and Analysis," *Annals of Behavioral Medicine* 49, no. 4 (August 2015): 542–56, ncbi.nlm.nih.gov/pmc/articles/PMC4498975.

7. T. J. Schoenfeld et al., "Physical Exercise Prevents Stress-Induced Activation of Granule Neurons and Enhances Local Inhibitory Mechanisms in the Dentate Gyrus," *Journal of Neuroscience* 33, no. 18 (May 1, 2013): 7770–77, ncbi.nlm.nih.gov/pubmed/23637169.

8. J. A. Smits et al., "Reducing Anxiety Sensitivity with Exercise," *Depression and Anxiety* 25, no. 8 (2008): 689–99, ncbi.nlm.nih.gov/pubmed/18729145.

9. Q. Tian et al., "Attentional Bias to Emotional Stimuli Is Altered During Moderate- but Not High-Intensity Exercise," *Emotion* 11, no. 6 (December 2011): 1415–24, ncbi.nlm.nih.gov/pubmed/21707164.

10. J. C. Smith, "Effects of Emotional Exposure on State Anxiety After Acute Exercise," *Medicine & Science in Sports & Exercise* 45, no. 2 (February 2013): 372–78, ncbi.nlm.nih.gov/pubmed/22895382.

Chapter 4: How to Use Running to Improve Your Mood

1. M. Guszowska, "Effects of Exercise on Anxiety, Depression and Mood," *Psychiatria Polska* 38, no. 4 (July–August 2004): 611–20, ncbi.nlm.nih.gov/pubmed/15518309.

2. A. A. Weinstein et al., "The Role of Depression in Short-Term Mood and Fatigue Responses to Acute Exercise," *International Journal of Behavioral Medicine* 17 (2010): 51–57, ncbi.nlm.nih.gov/pubmed/19333764.

3. H. Boecker, "The Runner's High: Opioiodergic Mechanisms in the Human Brain," *Cerebral Cortex* 18, no. 11 (November 2008): 2523–31, ncbi.nlm.nih.gov/pubmed/18296435.

4. David A. Raichlen et al., "Wired to Run: Exercise-Induced Endocannabinoid Signaling in Humans and Cursorial Mammals with Implications for the 'Runner's High,'" *Journal of Experimental Biology* 215 (2012): 1331–36, jeb.biologists.org/content/215/8/1331.

5. David A. Raichlen, "Exercise-Induced Endocannabinoid Signaling Is Modulated by Intensity," *European Journal of Applied Physiology* 113 (2013): 869–75, raichlen.arizona.edu/DavePDF/RaichlenEtAl2013.pdf.

6. T. Saanijoki et al., "Opioid Release After High-Intensity Interval Training in Healthy Human Subjects," *Neuropsychopharmacology* (July 19, 2017), ncbi.nlm.nih.gov/pubmed/28722022.

7. A. G. Brellenthin et al., "Endocannibinoid and Mood Responses to Exercise in Adults with Varying Activity Levels," *Medicine and Science in*

Sports and Exercise 49, no. 8 (August 2017): 1688–96, ncbi.nlm.nih.gov/pubmed/28319590.

8. R. Mitchell, "Is Physical Activity in Natural Environments Better for Mental Health Than Physical Activity in Other Environments?" *Social Science and Medicine* 91 (August 2013): 130–34, ncbi.nlm.nih.gov/pubmed/22705180.

9. Peter Aspinall et al., "The Urban Brain: Analyzing Outdoor Physical Activity with Mobile EEG," *British Journal of Sports Medicine* 49, no. 4, bjsm.bmj.com/content/49/4/272.

10. Jo Barton et al., "What Is the Best Dose of Nature and Green Exercise for Improving Mental Health? A Multi-study Analysis," *Environmental Science & Technology* 4, no. 10 (2010): 3947–55, pubs.acs.org/doi/abs/10.1021/es903183r.

11. I. Bos et al., "No Exercise-Induced Increase in Serum BDNF After Cycling Near a Major Traffic Road," *Neuroscience Letters* 500, no. 2 (2011): 129–32, ncbi.nlm.nih.gov/pubmed/21708224.

12. World Health Organization, "'Depression: Let's Talk' Says WHO, as Depression Tops List of Causes of Ill Health," press release, March 30, 2017, who.int/mediacentre/news/releases/2017/world-health-day/en.

13. J. B. Dyer et al., "Effects of Running and Other Activities on Moods," *Perceptual and Motor Skills* 67, no. 1 (August 1988): 43–50, ncbi.nlm.nih.gov/pubmed/3211691.

14. F. B. Schuch et al., "Are Lower Levels of Cardiorespiratory Fitness Associated with Incident Depression? A Systematic Review of Prospective Cohort Studies," *Preventive Medicine* (2016), ncbi.nlm.nih.gov/m/pubmed/27765659.

15. M. Reichert et al., "Exercise Versus Nonexercise Activity: E-diaries Unravel Distinct Effects on Mood," *Medicine & Science in Sports & Exercise* 49, no. 4 (April 2017): 763–73, ncbi.nlm.nih.gov/pubmed/27824691.

Chapter 5: Running and Antidepressants

1. Laura A. Pratt et al., "Antidepressant Use Among Persons Aged 12 and Over: United States, 2011–2014," NCHS Data Brief No. 283, August 2017, cdc.gov/nchs/products/databriefs/db283.htm.

2. Arif Khan et al., "Antidepressants Versus Placebo in Major Depression:

An Overview," *World Psychiatry* 14, no. 3 (October 2015): 294–300, ncbi. nlm.nih.gov/pmc/articles/PMC4592645.

3. F. Teixeira-Coelho et al., "The Paroxetine Effect on Exercise Performance Depends on the Aerobic Capacity of Exercising Individuals," *Journal of Sports Science & Medicine* 13, no. 2 (May 2014): 232–43, ncbi.nlm.nih .gov/pmc/articles/PMC3990874.

4. P. Watson et al., "Acute Dopamine/Noradrenaline Reuptake Inhibition Enhances Human Exercise Performance in Warm, but Not Temperate Conditions," *Journal of Physiology* 565, part 3 (June 15, 2005): 873–83, ncbi.nlm.nih.gov/pmc/articles/PMC1464564.

5. B. Roelands et al., "Performance and Thermoregulatory Effects of Chronic Bupropion Administration in the Heat," *European Journal of Applied Physiology* 105, no. 3 (February 2009): 493–98, ncbi.nlm.nih.gov/ pubmed/19002702.

6. A. T. Strachan et al., "Paroxetine Administration to Influence Human Exercise Capacity, Perceived Effort or Hormone Responses During Prolonged Exercise in a Warm Environment," *Experimental Physiology* (October 29, 2014), onlinelibrary.wiley.com/doi/10.1113/ expphysiol.2004.027839/full.

7. Ethan Ruderman, "Effects of Acute Aerobic Exercise on the Pharmacokinetics of the Anti-anxiety/Anti-depressant Drug Sertraline," TSpace Repository, December 10, 2013, tspace.library.utoronto.ca/ handle/1807/43322.

8. C. L. Reardon et al., "Psychiatric Medication Preferences of Sports Psychiatrists," *The Physician and Sportsmedicine* 44, no. 4 (November 2016): 397–402, ncbi.nlm.nih.gov/pubmed/27463033.

Chapter 6: Running and Talk Therapy

1. Alan J. Gelenberg et al., "Practice Guideline for the Treatment of Patients with Major Depressive Disorder," 3rd ed., American Psychiatric Association, 2010, psychiatryonline.org/pb/assets/raw/sitewide/practice_ guidelines/guidelines/mdd.pdf.

2. Evan Mayo-Wilson et al., "Psychological and Pharmacological Interventions for Social Anxiety Disorder in Adults: A Systematic Review and Network Meta-analysis," *The Lancet Psychiatry* 1, no. 5 (October 2014): 368–76, sciencedirect.com/science/article/pii/ S2215036614703293.

3. Steven D. Hollon et al., "Does Publication Bias Inflate the Apparent Efficacy of Psychological Treatment for Major Depressive Disorder? A Systematic Review and Meta-analysis of US National Institutes of Health-Funded Trials," *PLoS One* (September 30, 2015), journals.plos .org/plosone/article?id=10.1371/journal.pone.0137864.

Chapter 7: Running and Cognitive Behavioral Therapy

1. Ellen Driessen et al., "Cognitive Behavioral Therapy for Mood Disorders: Efficacy, Moderators and Mediators," *Psychiatric Clinics of North America* 33, no. 3 (September 2010): 537–55, ncbi.nlm.nih.gov/pmc/articles/ PMC2933381.

2. Stefan G. Hofmann et al., "Cognitive-Behavioral Therapy for Adult Anxiety Disorders: A Meta-analysis of Randomized Placebo-Controlled Trials," *Journal of Clinical Psychiatry* 69, no. 4 (2008): 621–32, psychiatrist.com/JCP/article/Pages/2008/v69n04/v69n0415.aspx.

3. Robert J. DeRubeis et al., "Cognitive Therapy Versus Medication for Depression: Treatment Outcomes and Neural Mechanisms," *Nature Reviews Neuroscience* 9, no. 10 (October 2008): 788–96, ncbi.nlm.nih. gov/pmc/articles/PMC2748674.

4. P. R. Porto et al., "Does Cognitive Behavioral Therapy Change the Brain? A Systematic Review of Neuroimaging in Anxiety Disorders," *Journal of Neuropsychiatry and Clinical Neurosciences* 21, no. 2 (Spring 2009): 114–25, ncbi.nlm.nih.gov/pubmed/19622682.

5. K. N. T. Månsson et al., "Neuroplasticity in Response to Cognitive Behavior Therapy for Social Anxiety Disorder," *Translational Psychiatry*, no. 6 (2016), nature.com/tp/journal/v6/n2/full/tp2015218a.html.

6. W. Freund et al., "Ultra-Marathon Runners Are Different: Investigations into Pain Tolerance and Personality Traits of Participants of the TransEurope FootRace 2009," *Pain Practice* 13, no. 7 (September 2013): 524–32, ncbi.nlm.nih.gov/pubmed/23368760.

7. N. Geva et al., "Enhanced Pain Modulation Among Triathletes: A Possible Explanation for Their Exceptional Capabilities," *Pain* 152, no. 11 (November 2013): 2317–23, ncbi.nlm.nih.gov/pubmed/23806655.

8. Matthew D. Jones et al., "Aerobic Training Increases Pain Tolerance in Healthy Individuals," *Medicine & Science in Sports & Exercise* 46, no. 8 (August 2014): 1640–47, journals.lww.com/acsm-msse/

Citation/2014/08000/Aerobic_Training_Increases_Pain_Tolerance_
in.21.aspx.

9. T. J. O'Leary et al., "High but Not Moderate-Intensity Endurance
    Training Increases Pain Tolerance: A Randomized Trial," *European
    Journal of Applied Physiology* 117, no. 11 (November 2017): 2201–10, ncbi.
    nlm.nih.gov/pubmed/28879617.

10. N. Geva et al., "Triathletes Lose Their Advantageous Pain Modulation
    Under Acute Psychosocial Stress," *Medicine & Science in Sports & Exercise*
    49, no. 2 (February 2017): 333–41, ncbi.nlm.nih.gov/pubmed/27669445.

Chapter 8: Running and Mindfulness

1. N. Geschwind et al., "Mindfulness Training Increases Momentary
    Positive Emotions and Reward Experience in Adults Vulnerable to
    Depression: A Randomized Controlled Trial," *Journal of Consulting and
    Clinical Psychology* 79, no. 5 (October 2011): 618–28, ncbi.nlm.nih.gov/
    pubmed/21767001.

2. S. G. Hofmann et al., "The Effect of Mindfulness-Based Therapy on
    Anxiety and Depression: A Meta-analytic Review," *Journal of Consulting
    and Clinical Psychology* 78, no. 2 (April 2010): 169–83, ncbi.nlm.nih.gov/
    pubmed/20350028.

3. Abdollah Omidi et al., "Comparing Mindfulness Based Cognitive
    Behavioral Therapy and Traditional Cognitive Behavior Therapy with
    Treatments as Usual on Reduction of Major Depressive Disorder
    Symptoms," *Iranian Red Crescent Medical Journal* 15, no. 2 (February
    2013): 142–46, ncbi.nlm.nih.gov/pmc/articles/PMC3652501.

4. Willem Kuyken et al., "Effectiveness and Cost-Effectiveness of
    Mindfulness-Based Cognitive Therapy Compared with Maintenance
    Antidepressant Treatment in the Prevention of Depressive Relapse
    or Recurrence: A Randomized Controlled Trial," *Lancet* 386, no.
    9988 (2015): 63–73, thelancet.com/journals/lancet/article/PIIS0140-
    6736(14)62222-4/abstract.

5. B. L. Alderman et al., "MAP Training: Combining Meditation and
    Aerobic Exercise Reduces Depression and Rumination While Enhancing
    Synchronized Brain Activity," *Translational Psychiatry* (February 2, 2016),
    nature.com/tp/journal/v6/n2/full/tp2015225a.html.

6. Kenneth E. Callen, "Auto-Hypnosis in Long Distance Runners,"

American *Journal of Clinical Hypnosis* 26, no. 1 (1983): 30–36, tandfonline.com/doi/abs/10.1080/00029157.1983 .10404135?journalCode=ujhy20.

7.   Lillian A. De Petrillo et al., "Mindfulness for Long-Distance Runners: An Open Trial Using Mindful Sport Performance Enhancement (MSPE)," *Journal of Clinical Sport Psychology* 3, no. 4 (2009): 357–76, journals .humankinetics.com/doi/abs/10.1123/jcsp.3.4.357; Darko Jekauc et al., "Effectiveness of a Mindfulness-Based Intervention for Athletes," *Psychology* 8, no. 1 (2017), file.scirp.org/Html/1-6902020_73192.htm.

8.   Rachel W. Thompson et al., "One Year Follow-up of Mindful Sport Performance Enhancement (MSPE) with Archers, Golfers, and Runners," *Journal of Clinical Sport Psychology* 5, no. 2 (2011): 99–116, journals .humankinetics.com/doi/10.1123/jcsp.5.2.99.

9.   Noel E. Brick et al., "Altering Pace Control and Pace Regulation: Attentional Focus Effects During Running," *Medicine & Science in Sports & Exercise* 48, no. 5 (May 2016): 879–86, ncbi.nlm.nih.gov/ pubmed/26673128.

10. Mihaly Csikszentmihalyi et al., *Running Flow: Mental Immersion Techniques for Better Running* (Champaign, IL: Human Kinetics, 2017), 6.

11. Cian Aherne et al., "The Effect of Mindfulness Training on Athletes' Flow: An Initial Investigation," *Sport Psychologist* 25, no. 2 (2011): 1770189, journals.humankinetics.com/doi/abs/10.1123/tsp.25.2.177.

Chapter 9: Running and Strong Social Connections

1.   J. T. Cacioppo et al., "Loneliness as a Specific Risk Factor for Depressive Symptoms: Cross-Sectional and Longitudinal Analyses," *Psychology and Aging* 21, no. 1 (March 2006): 140–51, www.ncbi.nlm.nih.gov/ pubmed/16594799.

2.   F. Holvast et al., "Loneliness Is Associated with Poor Prognosis in Late-Life Depression: Longitudinal Analysis of the Netherlands Study of Depression in Older Persons," *Journal of Affective Disorders* 185 (October 1, 2015): 1–7, ncbi.nlm.nih.gov/pubmed/26142687.

3.   Gillian A. Matthews et al., "Dorsal Raphe Dopamine Neurons Represent the Experience of Social Isolation," *Cell* 164, no. 4 (2016): 617–31, cell .com/cell/fulltext/S0092-8674(15)01704-3.

4.   K. A. Michelsen et al., "The Dorsal Raphe Nucleus and Serotonin: Implications for Neuroplasticity Linked to Major Depression and

Alzheimer's Disease," *Progress in Brain Research* 172 (2008): 233–64, ncbi.nlm.nih.gov/pubmed/18772036.

5. L. Y. Lin et al., "Association Between Social Media Use and Depression Among US Adults," *Depression and Anxiety* 33, no. 4 (April 2016): 323–31, ncbi.nlm.nih.gov/pubmed/26783723.

6. Brian A. Primack et al., "Social Media Use and Perceived Social Isolation Among Young Adults in the US," *American Journal of Preventive Medicine* 53, no. 1 (July 2017): 1–8, ajpmonline.org/article/S0749-3797(17)30016-8/abstract, http://www.ajpmonline.org/article/S0749-3797(17)30016-8/fulltext.

7. Christian J. Cook et al., "The Social Environment During a Post-match Video Presentation Affects the Hormonal Responses and Playing Performance in Professional Male Athletes," *Physiology & Behavior* 130 (May 2014): 170–75, sciencedirect.com/science/article/pii/S0031938414001802.

Chapter 11: Running and a Healthy Lifestyle

1. Felice N. Jacka et al., "A Randomized Controlled Trial of Dietary Improvement for Adults with Major Depression (The 'SMILES' Trial)," *BMC Medicine* 15 (2017): 23, bmcmedicine.biomedcentral.com/articles/10.1186/s12916-017-0791-y.

2. Simon Spedding, "Vitamin D and Depression: A Systematic Review and Meta-analysis Comparing Studies with and without Biological Flaws," *Nutrients* 6, no. 4 (April 2014): 1501–18, ncbi.nlm.nih.gov/pmc/articles/PMC4011048.

3. G. Grosso et al., "Coffee, Tea, Caffeine and Risk of Depression: A Systematic Review and Dose-Response Meta-analysis of Observational Studies," *Molecular Nutrition & Food Research* 60, no. 1 (January 2016): 223–34, ncbi.nlm.nih.gov/pubmed/26518745.

4. L. Wang et al., "Coffee and Caffeine Consumption and Depression: A Meta-analysis of Observational Studies," *Australian and New Zealand Journal of Psychiatry* 50, no. 3 (March 2016): 228–42, ncbi.nlm.nih.gov/pubmed/26339067.

5. Avin Muthuramalingam et al., "Is Depression an Inflammatory Disease? Findings from a Cross-sectional Study at a Tertiary Care Center," *Indian Journal of Psychological Medicine* 38, no. 2 (March–April 2016): 114–19,

ncbi.nlm.nih.gov/pmc/articles/PMC4820549.

6. N. Tsuno et al., "Sleep and Depression," *Journal of Clinical Psychiatry* 66, no. 10 (October 2005): 1254–69, ncbi.nlm.nih.gov/pubmed/16259539.

7. Peter L. Franzen, "Sleep Disturbances and Depression: Risk Relationships for Subsequent Depression and Therapeutic Implications," *Dialogues in Clinical Neuroscience* 10, no. 4 (December 2008): 473–81, ncbi.nlm.nih .gov/pmc/articles/PMC3108260.

8. H. S. Driver et al., "Exercise and Sleep," *Sleep Medicine Reviews* 4, no. 4 (August 2000): 387–402, ncbi.nlm.nih.gov/pubmed/12531177.

9. K. J. Reid et al., "Aerobic Exercise Improves Self-Reported Sleep and Quality of Life in Older Adults with Insomnia," *Sleep Medicine* 11, no. 9 (October 2010): 934–40, ncbi.nlm.nih.gov/pubmed/20813580.

10. Bridget F. Grant et al., "Prevalence and Co-occurrence of Substance Use Disorders and Independent Mood and Anxiety Disorders: Results from the National Epidemiologic Survey on Alcohol and Related Conditions," *Archives of General Psychiatry* 61, no. 8 (2004): 807–16, jamanetwork .com/journals/jamapsychiatry/fullarticle/482045.

11. A. K. Piazza-Gardner et al., "Examining Physical Activity Levels and Alcohol Consumption: Are People Who Drink More Active?" *American Journal of Health Promotion* 26, no. 3 (January-February 2012): 95–104, ncbi.nlm.nih.gov/pubmed/22208422.

12. D. E. Conroy et al., "Daily Physical Activity and Alcohol Use Across the Adult Lifespan," *Health Psychology* 34, no. 6 (June 2015): 653–60, ncbi .nlm.nih.gov/pubmed/25222084.

13. P. Christiansen et al., "Ego Depletion Increases Ad-Lib Alcohol Consumption: Investigating Cognitive Mediators and Moderators," *Experimental and Clinical Psychopharmacology* 20, no. 2 (April 2012): 118–28, ncbi.nlm.nih.gov/pubmed/22182418.

14. M. H. De Moor et al., "Regular Exercise, Anxiety, Depression and Personality: A Population-Based Study," *Preventive Medicine* 42, no. 4 (April 2006): 273–79, ncbi.nlm.nih.gov/pubmed/16439008.

Chapter 12: What Running Can and Can't Do

1. T. L. Greer et al., "Improvements in Psychosocial Functioning and Health-Related Quality of Life Following Exercise Augmentation in Patients with Treatment Response but Nonremitted Major Depressive Disorder: Results from the TREAD Study," *Depression and Anxiety* 33,

no. 9 (September 2016): 870–81. ncbi.nlm.nih.gov/pubmed/27164293.

2.   A. A. Weinstein et al., "Mental Health Consequences of Exercise
      Withdrawal: A Systematic Review," *General Hospital Psychiatry* (June 6,
      2017), ncbi.nlm.nih.gov/pubmed/28625704.

3.   H. K. Antunes et al., "Exercise Deprivation Increases Negative Mood in
      Exercise-Addicted Subjects and Modifies Their Biochemical Markers,"
      Physiology & Behavior 156 (March 15, 2016): 182-90, ncbi.nlm.nih.gov/
      pubmed/26812592.

ACKNOWLEDGMENTS

Several people, most of them strangers to me, talked openly about running to manage their mental health. Their candor inspired me to share more of my experiences.

Several experts on the various topics in the book endured my odd, rambling questions. Paddy Ekkekakis and Laura Fredendall were especially generous with their time and knowledge. It's been said that a book is a collection of pages containing at least one error. Any mistakes in this book are my fault, not the experts'.

This book's editor, Nicholas Cizek, was an absolute delight to work with throughout, starting with our first discussion (ninety minutes long!). Soon after that phone call, I met Nick and The Experiment's publisher, Matthew Lore, in their office, and knew I'd found the right home for the book I'd been thinking about for years.

Pete Magill introduced me to Nick and The Experiment, for which he's written two excellent running books.

Alison Wade provided the photos that open each chapter. To see more images that will make you want to get outside and run, follow Alison on Instagram @comeback_runner.

Allison Goldstein did an excellent job finding relevant research, no matter how esoteric the rabbit holes I sent her down. I hope we can work together again.

Two of my running partners, Kristin Barry and Julia Kirtland, patiently listened to me talk through topics in the book during our miles together.

Slowdive and Georg Philipp Telemann wrote the perfect music for regrouping during writing breaks.

Some of the reporting in this book previously appeared in *Runner's World*. Sarah Lorge Butler deftly edited that work. Most of this material has substantially changed, but there are a few places where the original sentences I wrote remained the best way I could think to phrase things.

Finally, I learned while writing this book that immersing yourself in its topics doesn't always lead to the best moods. My wife, Stacey Cramp, was even more forbearing and supportive than usual during this time. Stacey isn't responsible for my happiness, but she and running are the two main contributors to it.

ABOUT THE AUTHORS

SCOTT DOUGLAS is a contributing editor for *Runner's World*. He has also been the editor of *Running Times* and *Runner's World*'s news channel. Scott has written or cowritten eight other books, including the *New York Times* bestseller *Meb for Mortals* and perennial favorite *Advanced Marathoning*. He has run more than 110,000 miles since taking up the sport in 1979. Scott lives in South Portland, Maine.

Named by *Women's Running* as one of twenty women who are changing the sport of running and the world, foreword author **ALISON MARIELLA DÉSIR** is the founder of Harlem Run and Run 4 All Women, and hosts the podcast *Find Meaning (on the RUN)*.